STRICTLY PERSONAL

STRICTLY PERSONAL

Why Federal Agents Conspired To Frame An
Innocent Man And How They Got Away With It

JACK GAIL

with **PAUL GALLENDER**

For my parents

PREFACE

The moment I laid eyes on Bonnie Sharkey, I knew we were going to be married. I just didn't think it would take 35 years to happen. The chance meetings that trigger life-changing events are rarely as recognizable or as positive as love at first sight. Sometimes they can be downright disastrous and I've experienced more than my share of the latter.

It took 40 years before I fully understood the federal government's vicious and reprehensible persecution of me, and only after I decided to write a book about my experiences. Because I'm an ex-felon, no attorney would help clear my name and get my 1992 conviction vacated. Since I'll never get my case overturned in a court of law, I'll let the readers be my jurors.

INTRODUCTION

"Court is one of those places where facts still matter. If the people don't have the facts, democracy can't work."

Judge Amy Berman Jackson

I'VE ALWAYS BELIEVED that the Justice Department is the spine of the country and that it's supposed to protect every American. That being said, the job of federal agents and prosecutors is to turn people into rats, stool pigeons or informants, and they're rewarded with promotions that enhance their pensions and reputations. That's what our justice system has become and it's been that way for decades. I know this because I've had a front-row seat to that behavior and I've been victimized by it in a major way.

Most people would inform on others in a second if it meant staying out of jail or getting their sentences greatly reduced. The Feds try to take your soul but I'm one of the few people who refused to let anyone take mine. Because of that, I became a marked man in the eyes of the federal government for more than 25 years. Federal agents and prosecutors don't care that their behavior ruins the lives of people and the lives of their loved ones. They look down on people who betray others, but they despise the guys who don't. That's what makes it so personal to them. They get angry and they hold grudges. They want to cost you as much money and aggravation as they can and they do it with a vengeance. They enjoy destroying people and some of them love it.

A reputation takes a lifetime to build but a second to destroy. I paid a heavy price for one stupid mistake, but the agencies and people on the cover of this book didn't think it was punishment enough. I was never given a second chance, other than the chance to become a government informant, which to the Feds was my only option. Because I wouldn't flip on the guy who put me in prison, they made up their minds to punish me and they didn't care how they did it.

When FBI agents do something as mean-spirited and blatantly illegal as what they did to me, it's because no one is holding them accountable for their behavior. In 1977, FBI agents lied to protect themselves and they did so at the expense of my wife, my children, and me. But that wasn't good enough for the Feds, because the ATF pulled the same shit on me 15 years later, and they went for my jugular.

1

NEVER LET ANYONE GO HOME BROKE

MY FATHER MADE sure I was never exposed to any semblance of organized crime and there was never any talk of it when his classy Italian friends visited our house. To me, they were legitimate guys who took care of their families, helped other people, and never let anybody push them around. I grew up thinking that's how men were supposed to act and I wanted to be like them.

Bookmakers were businessmen trying to make a living, like my grandfather, Tommy. He and his partner had two bookie joints and two poker rooms, which were the Jewish men's clubs of the time. Tommy always made money, and he had a heart. The rule at his Westside bookie parlors was never let anyone go home to his wife broke. If a guy blew all his money betting on horses and playing poker, Tommy would drop a 10 or a 20 in his pocket when he left.

My father was a big help to his dad because he was really good with numbers. He worked full-time at his father's bookie joint after dropping out of high school. By the time he would have graduated, he could have run his own operation. Tommy always told my father if the police ever came when he wasn't there, he should just close up the place and go home. One Saturday, the place was packed when the police came and told my father to close up. He immediately got everybody to leave, walked outside, and watched the police drive away. People schmoozed for a few minutes until he said, "All right, everybody back inside, they ain't gonna come back." Well, they came back thirty minutes later and arrested my father.

People could hear my grandfather coming even before he opened the door to the police station. "Where is that fat cocksucker. You fat motherfucker, you lock up my kid, are you nuts?" Tommy was screaming at the Station Commander who promptly yelled, "Get that kid out of the cell!" What I love about that story is by the time my father got home, Tommy, the Commander, and two other guys were in the living room playing pinochle. That typified the kind of relationship organized crime and law enforcement used to enjoy. Payoffs were a cost of doing business to the Outfit, and a nice second income for people at all levels of law enforcement. Things stayed that way for many years because it benefited both parties.

Not everything about organized crime was negative. The mob helped build America, and they did it from the ground up. People all over the country wanted alcohol and gambling, and organized crime gave them both. Mob controlled businesses produced the concrete for every building in every major city in the country. More importantly, the Outfit financed thousands of small businesses and did it in a legitimate way, at least in Chicago.

Before and after World War II, five or ten thousand dollars is what it took to start a business, but money was hard to come by. The people the banks turned down got their stakes from the Outfit. They worked hard, paid off their loans, and spent the rest of their lives reaping the fruits of their labor. These weren't juice loans, they were build-the-future loans, and I knew a lot of people who got them. They took the opportunity the mob gave them to live the American dream and they were very grateful. The government called it corruption, but the people who benefited from it called it existing.

Joseph Kennedy supplied the mob with alcohol, but nobody ever talked about him being hooked up with organized crime. He got scotch from Scotland and unloaded it in Canada, which is where his involvement stopped. He wasn't breaking any laws in the United

States because everything he did was outside of the country. The Outfit took a short boat ride from Put-In-Bay Island in northern Ohio to Canada, and smuggled the alcohol into the U.S., mostly through Cleveland and Detroit. Back then, the police didn't have boats to patrol the waters and they didn't have any way to communicate with each other. If and when the police intercepted the shipments, they were paid to look the other way. Only God knows how much money they all made, but I doubt God had the time to count it. After all, Joe Kennedy made millions just for getting the product from point A to point B, and that was a fraction of what the mob made selling it.

For years, Tony Accardo was in charge of everything in Chicago. In my opinion, he was the boss of all bosses because of his genius. The average boss had a run of five or six years, and even that was a lot. The fate of organized crime bosses was similar to many Roman Emperors who had even shorter reigns. It's a lot more dangerous at the top than it is lonely, but Accardo reigned for 50 years and never spent a day in jail. If he got arrested, there was always a judge on his payroll who would drop whatever he was doing to get him released within the hour.

Accardo controlled the police, the courts and the key people in every area where the Outfit had interests. He was more powerful than the first Mayor Daley, which is saying a lot. Accardo brought Chicago to Las Vegas by getting the Teamsters to finance the purchase of the Stardust and Fremont properties. Tony Accardo was a genius not for what he did, but for how well he did it. The fact that he used his powers for evil darkens his accomplishments, but it doesn't diminish them. The mob controlled just about everything until the early 1990's when it effectively ceased to exist. The lawyers and the lobbyists took control of the system, and now you can't do anything in this country without a lawyer. God help us.

2
GROWING UP

MY PARENTS WERE married a month before we entered World War II. From what everybody told me, they were a great match with a great future. Betty was beautiful and had a heart of gold, and Lenny was a smart, likeable guy who always did the right thing. I was born shortly before my father shipped out to Italy in mid-1944, and he came home in 1946, ready to resume his life with my mother and me.

As fate would have it, Lenny Gail came home from a brutal war to face an even more terrifying reality. Less than a year later, my mother was pregnant with my brother, Steven, when she was diagnosed with Multiple Sclerosis. Dad soon found himself with two infant children and a young wife whose ability to function independently was disappearing day by day. My mother was wheelchair-bound by the age of 28 and I have little memory of her being out of that chair.

My father tried everything possible to help my mother, but when you get MS at 26, the nerve damage causes you to deteriorate very quickly. It's a truly terrible thing to watch, must less live through, and I had a ringside seat from the time I was four years old. Kids need days off, too, and though I can't recall ever having one, I was never unhappy. My existence involved taking care of my mother and helping my father in any way I could. There was always a positive atmosphere in our house because my father insisted on having a happy home.

After the war, Lenny knew he had to earn a living by doing something other than making book. The Outfit wanted him to continue taking bets, but he refused to do it. He got the opportunity he needed when three of his friends returned home from the war and began building houses. America was wide open for business and the suburbs fueled most of the population growth. Every home that his friends built would need tile and they told my father they'd buy all of theirs from him if he went into the business. That was America at its best, when friends wanted friends to do well and actually did something about it, rather than just wishing them well.

At one time, my father's company, Gail Tile & Carpet, Inc., had 100 employees. With all the building going on, I suggested that he purchase a house in every one of his friends' developments because they would be worth $10,000 more than what he paid for them as soon as construction was finished. He could have become a wealthy man, but he was satisfied with what he had. Like a lot of people who grew up during the depression, my father was afraid to take a risk.

In the mid-1950's we moved into a ranch house in Skokie that one of my father's friends had built. My dad bought the place for $19,000 and built a ramp to accommodate my mom's wheelchair. For years, people would come to our house to keep my mom company and take her for walks. I was always surrounded by people who were compassionate, loving, caring and helpful, and I've spent my life paying it forward. If I considered you a friend and you had a problem, I'd be the first one there to help.

I've been a protector all my life and I've saved the lives of five different people over the years. The first time I helped save a life was when I was 16. A woman was backing out of her driveway on Crawford Avenue in Skokie when a guy broadsided her and spun the car around until it came to rest on the median. Me and two friends were driving south on Crawford and we got there right after it happened.

We could see there was fire under the woman's car and we ran over to pull her out. Her car got hit so hard that the gas tank broke loose and came to a stop under the vehicle. She was a big woman and the force of the collision drove the entire front seat backwards, making it appear as though she was sitting in the back seat.

We helped the woman out of the car and walked her to the sidewalk, when she looked at me and said, "My purse is in the car!" I hesitated for a second but said to myself, "Alright, I can do this." I ran to the car, grabbed her purse and ran back to the sidewalk. At that moment, the entire car ignited and went up in flames. Only a kid would do what I did and it was one of very few times in my life that I got lucky. I shudder to think what would have happened to that woman had my friends and I not come by when we did. She was the real lucky one.

In 2015, I was having lunch with my father's 94-year-old best friend, when he started to choke on a hot dog. I performed the Heimlich maneuver on him and the hot dog popped out, but his gurgling told me there was still more food in his windpipe. We were 10 miles from any hospital but there was a firehouse four blocks away and that's where I took him. The firefighters put him in an ambulance and took him to the emergency room where a doctor removed the food from his esophagus. They told him he was lucky he didn't die.

My mother taught me an important life lesson that kids usually learn from their fathers. I was in the third grade when a big fat kid named Billy pushed me around in the cloak room. After Billy did that a second time, I asked my mother why he kept doing it. "He's a bully," she said, "and you should push him back." The next day, I waited for Billy to push me and when he did, I punched him in the face as hard as I could. He stopped pushing me after that and I never let anyone bully or disrespect me again. I suspect it's a little unusual that both of my parents gave me the confidence to fight my own battles, but they both did, and it served me well.

I had to fight my way through high school, but I only punched someone if I had a good reason. I never started fights but I didn't walk away from them either. I couldn't understand why bikers always wanted to fight me. I'd accidentally bump into somebody and he'd say, "I'll meet you after school." Even when I apologized, I got the same response. There were a lot of those guys back then and they learned not to mess with me, thanks in large part to the advice I got from my mother.

One day I came home from high school with blood on my shirt. My father asked me what happened and I said, "It's not my blood." Dad knew I never went looking for fights and that I always let the other guy throw the first punch. I never kicked a guy when he was down, and I never used anything other than my fists to hit him. Another time, a guy was making fun of a girl with cerebral palsy in the high school cafeteria. I asked him to stop and he wouldn't. Other kids tried to get him to stop but he wouldn't. He actually thought it was funny. I punched him in the face so hard that he fell backward into a coke machine and slid down to the floor, and he was out cold. When he made fun of that girl, I felt like he was making fun of my mother, which one idiot actually did.

I remember my mother complaining about her teeth. One of my father's best friends was a dentist who came over on a Sunday morning to examine her. Mom needed about two hours of dental work and he suggested they do it in a hospital where she'd be more comfortable lying down than sitting in a dentist chair. My dad dropped us off and went to park the car. As I was trying to maneuver my mom and her wheelchair at the same time, she fell backwards and I caught her. Just then, a guy walked by and said, "Take that drunk home!" I don't know why he chose to be an asshole at that particular moment, but it wasn't a well thought out idea. I sat my mother down on the grass and told her I'd be right back. Then I walked over to the guy and knocked him out with one punch.

As it turned out, that prick had a better day than my mother did. She died on the table at the same time that a heart specialist came by to say hello to the dentist. He brought her back by massaging her heart, but she was gone for over four minutes and spent the last year of her life in a vegetative state. Betty Gail passed away at the age of 39.

My father remarried less than a year after my mother died. He deserved happiness as much as anyone else, but life had afforded him very little of it from the moment he went to war. He and his second wife had known each other all their lives, and I knew her family, too. It would have been hard to find a woman as selfish as she was and I couldn't wait to leave home and get away from her, so I enlisted in the Army on my 18th birthday.

I was home on leave before being sent to South Korea for the last 13 months of my three-year commitment. My father asked me to pick up our dinner at The Cork Restaurant in Skokie. A good friend of my father owned the place and a lot of wiseguys hung out there. As my girlfriend and I were walking out with our food, we saw two guys in their forties fighting in the parking lot. The owner was pleading with a short, stocky guy with a long cigar in his mouth, to get them to stop. When they didn't, I told my girlfriend to hold on to the food.

All of a sudden, the short stocky guy said, "Okay, knock it off and go back inside." They immediately stopped fighting and were walking toward the door when the big guy called the little guy a cocksucker and went to push him. I put my hand on his arm and said, "Why don't you listen to the man and go back inside?" I didn't grab him, I just got his attention. All of a sudden I got pushed into a brick wall. I turned around and saw it was the short stocky guy who had pushed me. I picked him up and threw him on the hood of a car and slapped him five or six times. I said, "Who the fuck are you pushing?" The owner said, "Jackie, you don't know what you're doing. Leave him alone." As I was walking away, the little guy said, "Hey kid, when you see your old man, tell him you wanted to go up against Boodie." "Went up against?" I said, as I turned back toward him. "You can't fight worth shit!" The owner jumped between us and said, "Jackie, please get out of here, just go home!"

When I got home, my girlfriend told my father that something happened at the Cork. She said, "a little guy said Jack should tell you he wanted to go up against Boodie." I was in the kitchen and dad had an uneasy smile on his face when he said, "I heard you met Boodie." When I told my father I slapped him around, he said, "You actually slapped Boodie Cowan? Jackie, don't tell me that. Do you know who he is? He's a juice collector for the Outfit and he's part of the toughest crew on the north side of Chicago." Boodie worked for Lenny Patrick who, along with Rocky Potenza, were the bosses of the north side, and nobody did what I did to Boodie Cowan without suffering the consequences.

The next night my father told me he got a phone call from Boodie and I asked him what he said. "He said what a smart punk kid I had." My father went to the Cork the following day and was pleasantly surprised when the owner told him what had taken place in the parking lot. Knowing that I wasn't the cause of the situation, he arranged for a sit down with Boodie. They knew each other as kids and were in the Army together, and they never had a problem. My father wasn't afraid of too many people, but guys like Boodie Cowan always retaliated from insults, real or perceived. Dad could have gone to any number of people for help but he went directly to Boodie. "Why are you calling my kid a punk?" my father said. "You're the one who pushed him into a wall. You deserve what you got." They parted friends and wrote the whole thing off.

A few months after I was honorably discharged, my father and I went to the Black Angus on Western & Touhy to celebrate my return. The Black Angus was the place to be if you were anyone or anything in Chicago's Jewish community. A friend of mine was sitting at a nearby table and he said, "Jackie, you know my uncle?" I said, "I don't think so." He said, "Ralphie Greenberg, meet Jackie Gail." I went to shake his hand and he stuck his finger between my eyes and said, "You're the kid we almost left one night." I didn't say anything, but I saw Ralphie wink at my father as we went to sit down. Later, when I stood up to leave, Ralphie came over and put his arm around me. I said, "Take your damn hands off of me," and he started laughing. "Come here kid," he said. "I want to talk to you."

Ralphie Greenberg was a very rough guy. They called him the Jewish Jack Dempsey and he was part of Boodie's crew. "Jackie," he said, "I was there the night you put Boodie on that car. I razzed him for an hour after that. I said to him, 'You let a punk kid do that to you?'" I made Boodie look bad in front of his crew and that kind of thing always triggered an angry response. Rocky Potenza was at the Cork that night, too, and when he saw me throw Boodie on the hood of the car, he told Ralphie and another guy to go leave me in an alley. Ralphie said, "That's Lenny Gail's kid. He's a good kid, leave him alone." Ralphie saved me from a serious beating that day because of the respect that he and everybody else had for my father.

3

GREAT TIMES

IN LATE 1966, I was working for my father when I learned that construction had begun on the Tiara, a 30-story Condominium building on Sheridan Road. I went to the site to sell some tile and that's when I met Dominic Santarelli. He was 29 and looked and acted like a Hollywood leading man. He was one of the classiest guys I ever met and had a personality second to none. I've always been impressed by talent, and Dominic had it in spades. He began building two-flats in his early '20s and worked his way up to 64-unit apartment buildings in less than five years. The Tiara was part of the Chicago skyline before he turned 30.

I told Dominic I was there to bid on the building's tile and carpet contract and we hit if off immediately. He invited me to lunch and we laughed through most of it. We talked about people we both knew and he told me to give him a formal proposal. We were already great friends by the time he gave Gail Tile the job a few weeks later. Dominic and I were inseparable for the next three years and I didn't have a better friend than him. He'd come to my father's house for Passover Seders, and we'd go to his mother's house for her fabulous Italian dinners. She made Sunday Gravy, which Italian women used to make every Sunday. Today, it's called sauce, but that word doesn't do it justice.

The rapport Dominic and I had was rare because you don't find guys with similar personalities who got along as well as we did. We never competed with each other, except when we were picking up women, and we went everywhere together. He took me to clubs where mob figures hung out and that's where I was first introduced to members of organized crime.

In February, 1967, two feet of snow paralyzed the city of Chicago and it took us four days to get a flight to Ft. Lauderdale. One of Dominic's friends introduced us to Rocky Marciano and a few hours later, we were having dinner with the undefeated Heavyweight Champion of the World. Rocky was America's champ and the pride of all Italians. My father was convinced that more people wanted to meet Marciano than had wanted to meet President Kennedy, and I think he was right.

I loved going out to dinner with Rocky. Restaurants always served us the best food, gave us the best service, seated us at the best tables, and never gave us a check. Before we returned home, I told Rocky to let Dominic and I know when he was coming to Chicago, and invited him to stay with us. He came to town a couple of months later and asked me to drive him wherever he needed to go. I met the world hanging with Rocky Marciano, because the world, including organized crime figures, flocked to him. To most wiseguys, Rocky was the best character reference a 23-year-old guy could have.

Rocky had a dry sense of humor, but he wasn't a funny person. He didn't open up to people unless he felt comfortable with them, and he wouldn't joke around unless he knew you and liked you. Rocky and I would occasionally do some non-contact sparring and he'd pretend to be hitting me on the arms. He told me his secret strategy was to hit his opponent's arms over and over until they went numb. After a few rounds of constant pounding, opponents had trouble lifting their arms, much less punching with them.

The moment Rocky stepped in the ring, his mindset was such that he wasn't going to lose, no matter who he was fighting. I saw his killer instinct when I watched films of his fights. The killer instinct isn't so much the look on a guy's face as it is the feeling that's in his heart. It's a quality that's easier to spot if you're a fighter like I was, but it's difficult to see if you're not. And let's be real here. You don't go 49-0, with 43 knockouts, by entering the ring thinking you're going to lose.

When turtlenecks came into style in 1968, I bought them in several different colors. One day I couldn't find my black one and I asked Dominic if he had seen it. He looked at me like I was crazy and said, "Who was just here?" That's when it hit me that Rocky had taken my sweater. The champ would "borrow" things from people because he didn't travel with luggage. The next time Rocky came to town, he said, "Hey pal, I left a shirt in your closet the last time I was here. Can I have it back?" I told him I'd give him back his shirt when he returned my black turtleneck. When Rocky looked to Dominic for help, he was told, "Fight your own battles."

In the two-and-a-half years I knew Rocky, I asked him to do me one favor. The son of one of my father's best friends was like a little brother to me. Tragically, Jeffrey developed a brain tumor at the age of nine. They operated and thought they got it all, but the tumor came back when he was 14. Two years later, it was clear that the end was near. I knew Rocky was Jeffrey's idol, and the day before his next visit, I called Jeffrey's father and told him I'd come by to get him at 10 a.m. so he could spend the day with us.

When we got to the airport, wooden-barricades were blocking access to the area where I needed to park. There was an Italian policeman standing there and I told him we were picking up Rocky Marciano. The cop started moving the barricades so fast that Jeffrey and I cracked up laughing. As I walked Rocky out of the airport, I told him Jeffrey's story and he thanked the cop who let me park there. We spent the entire day with Dominic and his family whose house had a huge, Olympic-size indoor pool with an indoor cabana where you could shower and change. Rocky treated Jeffrey like he was his own kid and he didn't leave his side until his dad picked him up at 10 that night.

I'm pretty sure Jeffrey thought about the time he spent with Rocky Marciano every day for the last six months of his life. It may have been the best day of his life because I was there, and it was one of the best days of my life. Jeffrey was 17 when he passed, and his father never forgot what I did for his son that day. In retrospect, I would have been better off if he had. More on that later.

That wasn't the only time I saw Rocky's big heart. Joe Kellman owned Globe Glass and was extremely successful. Kellman's companies made millions of dollars once he got all the insurance companies in the midwest to give him their glass replacement contracts for both autos and, later, buildings. He founded the Better Boys Foundation and held a benefit at the Sherman House in downtown Chicago for former heavyweight champ, Ezzard Charles. Rocky defended his title twice against Charles and a lot of people felt those two fights were the reason why Ez ended up in a wheelchair. Rocky, Jersey Joe Walcott, Archie Moore and Muhammad Ali were seated on the dais, as was Kellman's good friend, Mayor Daley. I was at my father's table.

When we left the dinner, a man on the sidewalk said his young friend would love to have Rocky's autograph, and pointed to a boy in a wheelchair across the street. I'll never forget the sight of the undefeated heavyweight champion of the world dodging traffic on LaSalle Street to shake a disabled kid's hand. Whatever you think of Rocky Marciano, you should know that he was worthy of your admiration and respect, both in and out of the ring.

I had been married a little more than two months when Rocky's plane crashed on its way to Des Moines, Iowa, on Labor Day weekend in 1969. He was to be the guest speaker at an Italian-American social club dinner, and the boss of St. Louis sent his son on a small plane to pick him up. The son had changed his last name which was why very few people knew that the son of the boss of St. Louis had died in that crash, too.

Rocky asked me and Dominic to come with him and I would have gone if I were still single. Dominic couldn't go either but he drove Rocky to Midway Airport. Rocky's wife Barbara called Dominic to tell him about the crash, and his first call was to me. Rocky's death was a huge loss for anyone who knew or admired him. For a long time, people told me I would have been on that plane if I hadn't gotten married, and they were absolutely right.

4
MY REPUTATION

I'VE ALWAYS SAID I was born too late. I would have rather come of age in the 1930's and 1940's when organized crime controlled almost everything in Chicago. The thing I liked most about the Life was the respect you were shown when you acted like a man. There was never any violence in my life. I was never part of a crew, I never muscled anyone, and nobody ever got hurt by dealing with me. It was a hell of a ride and the fringe benefits were great. I got the best tables at restaurants and the best seats at plays, concerts and sporting events. I drank the best scotch, wore the best clothes, I drove the best cars and lived in the penthouse of a 30-story building on Sheridan Rd. It was pretty cool stuff for a young man in his early twenties, and I thought it was going to remain that way forever.

Crews in the Chicago Outfit were different than those in other cities because of the way they carried themselves and how they talked. Wiseguys in Chicago never came on strong like New Yorkers did. New Yorkers acted and talked like caricatures of themselves and it was hard for me not to laugh at them. It may have been an act but I didn't have an act. What you saw was what you got and if I told you something, you could bank on it. Everyone knew that about me.

I was a fixer, and I always felt like I could get anything done. If somebody had a problem, I went and straightened it out. That's the reputation I enjoyed and people took notice. The oldtimers had me mediate situations that needed to be resolved in a rational, logical manner, and I made sure that the disappointed party never walked away mad. I never played favorites because my job was to solve problems, rather than create them.

When I responded to situations in a serious manner, people would notice that I had a look. That's something people have told me all my life, so I know it's true. I used to tell guys I'd play the game any way they wanted to play it. If they wanted to play it nice, we'd play it nice, but if someone wanted to be a jagoff, then we'd play it that way. I made sure they knew the decision was *theirs* to make, but incidents like that didn't happen very often. Most people never saw that side of me. What they saw was a confident guy with a sense of humor, and the courage to use it in any circumstances.

This particular story is the kind of thing upon which reputations were built in the Outfit. Felix "Milwaukee Phil" Alderisio may have been the most feared man in the United States in the 1960's. He served under Sam Giancana and became Chicago's street boss for a short time before going to prison, where he died. Dominic was friends with Phil, whose crew would hang out at the penthouse. Phil always brought opera albums with him and we'd have to listen to them whether we liked opera or not.

We'd have lunch with Phil and our girlfriends on Sundays, and one day he asked me and Dominic to pick up some beef at Carm's Beef Stand, which was the best in town. While we were eating, Dominic noticed that Phil was only eating sausage that day. "Why don't you try the beef," he asked. Phil said, "I don't want any." I don't know why that bothered Dominic, but he couldn't leave it alone. Five minutes later he said, "Come on Phil, eat the beef. I cooked it all morning." Phil looked at him in a way that made the tension in the room palpable. I was sitting next to him and I slammed my plate with a fork and growled, "Did he tell you to eat the beef? Then eat the beef!" Dominic jumped out of his chair and said, "Are you crazy, Jackie? You can't talk to Phil like that. Nobody talks to Phil like that." In the meantime, everyone broke up laughing, and Phil was fond of me after that. As a matter of fact, everyone in the room looked at me differently from that day forward. The way I handled myself gave people the impression that I had been born into the Life and was comfortable in my own skin.

Once the Outfit knew I could be trusted, they sent me to pick up and deliver large sums of their money. Every month I'd go to a certain hotel at the airport and pick up a paper bag containing $100,000 and bring it to somebody. I looked in the bag one time to make sure it didn't contain any drugs. There was just cash and I never looked in one of those bags again. I didn't ask any questions, either.

I was sent to other cities to bring back money for Chicago. In Baltimore, I went to a bar and was taken downstairs into a tunnel that emptied into a room where five shoe boxes were waiting for me. Each box contained $100,000 and was secured with string. The boxes were stacked on top of each other and tied together. I'd fly back to Chicago with half a million in cash on the seat next to me. Anytime I was asked to do something, I did it. The guys in charge weren't keen on giving second chances. Correct me if I'm wrong, but if you can't trust somebody to make a simple delivery, you can't trust him to do anything.

Dominic was close to the boss of Baltimore and whenever he came to Chicago, he'd visit us at the penthouse. One day, Dominic went to the bathroom and the boss leaned over to me and pointed to the sailfish mounted above the fireplace. In his heavy Sicilian accent, he said, "Jack, you know how that fish got uppa dere?" I said no and he replied, "He got uppa dere cuz he opened uppa hisa mouth." He smiled, and I nodded. "Now, when you do a somethin' by you self, that's a one a person who knows, right? Right! And when you do a somethin' with a someone else, that'sa two a persons who know, right?" He smiled, and I shook my head, no. "Good, cuz that'sa wrong. It's 11 a persons who willa know that. And when you do a somethin' with a third a person, it's 111 a people who willa know." He was telling me that bad things happen when people open their mouths and I never forgot his advice, or the manner in which he gave it to me.

The reputation I built for myself over a ten-year period made me one of the most respected guys in the city of Chicago. I had carved out my own niche and I was as independent as one could be in that world. I had earned the trust of the people who mattered most and my future could not have been brighter. I thought the Life would never end, but it had already begun to fall apart.

The federal government's plan to destroy organized crime started with RICO, the Racketeer Influenced and Corrupt Organizations Act. RICO gave Feds the ability to infiltrate organized crime, and to charge the bosses for the crimes they ordered others to commit. Guys found guilty of racketeering could be sentenced to 20 years in prison for each count, and forced to forfeit their personal and business assets. The government gave wiseguys two compelling reasons to cooperate with them. First, they didn't want to go to jail, much less die there, and, second, they didn't want to bankrupt their families. A lot of older guys were looking at life sentences no matter what their crimes were, and that's why they started flipping. Organized crime would never be the same.

The Italians used to take an oath of Omerta, meaning nobody talked. Well, it turned out that everybody talked. Systems break down when people don't play by the rules and that's what happened to the mob. Wiseguys stopped being men a long time ago, and they turned on each other when they realized their ass was on the line. There used to be a standing joke that when a crew got arrested, it was a race to the prosecutor's office, and the prosecutor had to slap 'em to get 'em to shut up. Most wiseguys became cooperators, and a lot of so-called tough guys showed the world they weren't so tough after all.

Betrayal puts more people in prison than anything else, and so it came to pass that the betrayers brought down the entire organized crime apparatus. The street economy dried up all over the country. Guys were afraid to talk to other guys because they didn't know if anyone else was listening to the conversation. The mob hastened their own demise when guys started doing cocaine in the '70s. They got caught up in the whole drug culture, like who had the most expensive straw. They lost control of themselves and everything went to shit.

The federal government couldn't have been happier because an agent's main source of information was, and continues to be, getting guys to inform on each other. It turned out to be the Achilles Heel of organized crime and developing a stable of informants became a cottage industry for the Federal government. Once a wiseguy flipped, the Feds owned him, and if his cover was blown, the Feds protected him. More than 10,000 people have been in the Witness Protection Program since the early 1970's, which works out to about five new informants a week. To paraphrase the old *Roach Motel* commercial, "CI's check in, but they don't check out."

When Michael Cohen agreed to cooperate with the Feds, President Trump suggested that flipping should be illegal. For a guy who thinks telling the truth should be illegal, it didn't come as much of a surprise to me. Trump knows that betrayal destroyed the mob, and he's scared to death that it's going to destroy him and his mob, too. Cohen should be scared for a different reason. He's going to rue the day that he flipped, and it's going to eat him alive. It doesn't matter if the guy he informed on was President Trump or Joe Shmoe. When you rat on people by testifying against them, it eats away at your soul. When Michael Cohen gets out of prison, he will have aged noticeably and his hair will probably be turning gray. However, the biggest difference in him will be something you can't see.

5

MY EDUCATION

I MET MY first wife early in 1969 and we got married in June. Our daughter was born nine months and six days after the wedding. When my father-in-law came to the hospital, I told him I knew he was counting. I had never heard of Frank Zimmerman and that wasn't by accident. Guys like Frank ran everything in Chicago but most people didn't have a clue about them.

Frank was as strong as they get, a real knock 'em out Jewish kid, admired and respected by everybody. He was a smart, class act guy who rarely talked, but he was a great listener. When Frank and Tony Accardo talked on the phone, they spoke in code, which everyone did at one time or another. My father-in-law liked working on cars and when he and Accardo spoke of carburetors, spark plugs, brake pads, and stick shifts, the FBI agents who were listening to the call had no idea what they were talking about. That's how the world worked back then and most of the guys who ran it were born before 1920. That's why we called them oldtimers, but never to their faces.

Frank would go to the Lawson YMCA five days a week to workout. He used to throw 60-yard passes to Chicago Bears receivers during their workouts. He could lay on his back and keep his feet off the ground for 10 minutes, which he was able to do into his '70's. I don't know anybody who could do that. However, my favorite Frank Zimmerman story involved his wife, Selma. She used to play bridge with Clarice Accardo and two other women who were married to the top people in Chicago. They always stopped playing at a quarter to ten. When it snowed, Frank would drive to wherever their game was, sweep the snow off Selma's car, start the engine and turn on the heat so all she had to do was unlock her warmed-up car and drive home. I never heard of any guy doing something like that for his wife and it made me want to be a better man. I'm afraid I fell short of that standard with my first wife.

I first realized how connected my father-in-law was when my wife and I went to Vegas. We were in our room at the Stardust when we got a call from the casino manager, Bobby Stella. Bobby was a big deal in Vegas and was the inspiration for the Don Rickles character in the movie, *Casino*. He said he heard I was a great guy and I shouldn't hesitate to ask if we needed anything, anything at all. He invited Harriet and I to have coffee with him and said he'd show us around the casino.

My wife wanted to play Baccarat and the pit boss started to teach her the game. I asked Mr. Stella to give her a $1,000 marker and he asked me if I had $1,000 in my pocket. I nodded, and he said, "Good, that's what you use. You can't have a marker here." He was looking out for us by saying that, and I was impressed. I knew very well that people can get carried away with their betting but Bobby wasn't going to let that happen to us. He was showing respect to my father-in-law by protecting his daughter, and he showed me what a classy guy he was in the process. Bobby wanted us to go home happy, but more than anything else, he didn't want us to get hurt. Life is all about who you are and who you know, and I suspect it's been that way as long as human beings have inhabited this planet.

Somebody told me a kid from Chicago was winning almost $120,000 shooting craps at the Stardust. It would be like winning three quarters of a million dollars today. Mr. Stella walked up to him and said, "Pick up your chips and go home." The kid said, "What are you talking about?" Bobby said, "Pick up your chips and go home.

Your father is a friend of mine." The kid said, "I'm winning!" and he started to argue. Once again, but with greater firmness, Bobby said, "Pick up your chips and go home. It's *enough!*" Turns out the kid's father was a well-known Chicago bookmaker and a highly respected guy. If this kid was a nobody, Bobby would have gladly let him lose back all that money, which he almost certainly would have done. Instead, the kid bought a house with his winnings and banked the rest, and his father called Stella to thank him for what he had done. That's how that world worked back then. Everybody knew everybody and they looked out for each other.

Federal agencies have always characterized Las Vegas in a negative light but credit should be given where credit is due. Ben Siegel, Meyer Lansky and the other guys who put Las Vegas together were geniuses who had the foresight to realize what they had, and what it could become. It was Tony Accardo who got the Teamsters Pension Fund to loan the Outfit $650 million for Las Vegas, an amount which was nothing compared to what they actually built.

You don't create a glamorous, cash business like Vegas by bringing together a bunch of conmen. Most of the hundreds of guys who were brought in to run the hotels and casinos were businessmen, rather than gangsters. The bosses created a foolproof way to generate vast sums of cash and they made everybody happy by giving pieces of the pie to all the big cities. This was competence in capital letters.

Then Tony Spilotro (Joe Pesci's character in *Casino*) and his crew moved to Vegas and started robbing everyone and everything. He actually flew into the Feds' radar, rather than under it. I can say with absolute certainty that nobody was ever sent to Las Vegas to rob people or do anything illegal, apart from skimming off the top. You don't have to rob people when they're willing to give you their money, and it already came in faster than the casinos could count it. By the way, Spilotro wasn't sent to Vegas to look out for Lefty Rosenthal. He left Chicago because there was so much damn heat on him. His leaving solved one problem for the Outfit, but it created a far greater one.

Spilotro ended up ruining things for wiseguys all over the country because he played by his own set of rules. I thought the oldtimers were too smart to let someone like Tony blow the whole thing up, but they did. The bosses got their money and looked the other way until it was too late to stop the implosion. When things started to fall apart in Vegas, Tony never blamed himself because guys who screw up always want to blame someone else. I was told a long time ago that anytime someone points a finger at you, there's always three fingers pointing back at him. The big corporations would have assumed control of Vegas at some point, but it would have taken a lot longer to happen if Spilotro had never gone there.

Las Vegas was part of a bigger picture that nobody talks about anymore. Most of the legal gambling in this country was learned from the mob, with the exception of bingo, which was God's gift to the churches and the manufacturers of folding chairs. The numbers racket morphed into lotteries. Off-track betting parlors replaced the kind of bookie joints that my grandfather Tommy ran. After Vegas and Cuba, casinos sprang up all over the country. Native Americans were given the right to operate casinos as a payoff for decades of genocide. Now that the Supreme Court has ruled that every state can allow gambling, don't be surprised if all of them do. Just be aware that organized crime gave America almost all of its gambling, but as far as I know, nobody ever thanked them.

My wife told me her father wanted us to come to his house when we got back from Vegas, so I knew something must be up. Once we were alone, Frank asked me if I would put my name on his restaurant's business and liquor licenses because he couldn't use his own name. They make it tough on felons who try to work their way back into society and even a connected guy like my father-in-law faced some obstacles which he couldn't surmount by going through normal channels. One of the guys fronting for him got indicted, and the city closed up the restaurant. They took away his liquor license, and you couldn't have a successful restaurant business without one. I was surprised when Frank made me the offer because he hadn't known me very long at the time. I told him I'd be happy to do that for him and he said, "The place is yours. Anything you make out of it is yours." The most important thing to Frank was having a place to hang out and hold court.

One day in the restaurant, a group of Italians were looking at me and one of them said, "You know, Jack, you are the man!" I said, "What do you mean?" He told me when Frank's restaurant closed, lots of guys told my father-in-law they knew people who could run the place, and every time they did, he told them, "I already got the guy." I could do no wrong in my father-in-law's eyes. Even after my wife and I split up, Frank and I remained close. A good friend of mine said I was the only ex-husband he ever knew whose father-in-law still had his back after the marriage to his daughter ended.

I named the new place, Civic Restaurant and Lounge. The restaurant could seat 250 people and had a nice sized bar. We were open from six in the morning to seven at night and we were always packed at lunchtime. Civic was located on LaSalle Street, a block and a half north of City Hall and a block and a half south of Traffic Court. The location made Civic a perfect meeting place for lawyers, prosecutors and judges, and a lot of business was conducted there. The restaurant served as a drop-off point where envelopes were passed to police commanders. The Outfit owned everyone back then and I hand-delivered a lot of those envelopes myself. You could get anything done in the City of Chicago if you could afford to pay for it, or if you had the right connections.

After a couple of years, I had an epiphany about the restaurant. I realized there wasn't a single Vienna hot dog joint in the Loop, nor was there a place selling Italian beef sandwiches. Those were Chicago's favorite sandwiches, as any Windy City native knows. If I extended my serving counter to the kitchen, it would have functioned like the cafeteria-style counter at Manny's Deli near Roosevelt Rd. I was pretty sure we could triple the restaurant's business because the foot traffic was already there and I'd be giving people what they wanted.

I thought it was one of my better ideas, but when I told Frank about it, he said no. He didn't have to tell me the reason because I already knew. Frank didn't want to change the character of the restaurant and my expansion plans would have definitely done that. He didn't care about growing the business because he wasn't in it for the money. Ultimately, it was Frank's decision to make and I didn't question it.

Three years later, one of my busboys ran up to me and said water was pouring out of a huge hole in the basement where we kept our supplies. There was so much water that I couldn't make it down all the stairs. There were rats everywhere, too. In little more than the blink of an eye, the restaurant was ancient history. I ran back upstairs with the rats hot on my trail, apologized to the customers and employees, and chased everyone out of the restaurant.

I called the Chicago Health Department to tell them about the situation and I gave them the landlord's phone number. Then I called the landlord and told him this was his problem and I was walking away from the lease. I emptied the cash register, got the checkbook and payroll records from the office, and locked the door behind me. I felt bad for the rats because once you've tasted good Jewish deli, it's difficult to live without it.

6

NOTHING LASTS LONG

I FELL INTO a lot of opportunities because of the guys I was around. Not everything I did to make a living was legal, but I never put anybody at risk. I picked up juice money on a few occasions, but I didn't like the way guys would get nervous when I showed up. A couple of times I walked in and the guy handing me money would be shaking. I'd say, "Why are you shaking?" and he'd say, "I don't want any trouble." I don't think he believed me when I told him he wasn't going to have any.

Another guy said, "Jack, I'm short," and I said, "Well, when will you have it?" He said he needed two weeks, so I told him I'd put up my own money and he could pay me on my next visit. Based on his personal experience, the guy thought I was gonna be angry, but beating somebody up over a few hundred dollars never made sense to me. Mobsters did it all the time because they trafficked in fear, and that's why the guy expected me to be a violent person. It didn't take long before I realized that line of work wasn't for me.

I never stole anything but people who did would bring me their stuff to sell. If you fenced stolen merchandise, you sold it for 50% of wholesale. I made a lot of money on truck tires for about a year, thanks to a guy in the trucking business who offered to have his drivers drop off their trucks anyplace I wanted. Truck tires were very expensive. Guys in the business wouldn't blink when I offered them the deal, and most of them took as many tires as they could get. I kept a fourth of what I got from the tire guys and cut up the rest.

I was involved with pinball machines for a couple of years. Back then, there were a lot of arcades. The Outfit had pinballs in thousands of locations and you couldn't be in that business without the backing of the mob. They put their own cigarette machines in those places, too, and all of it was tightly controlled, just like it was in every major American city. Their warehouse was an unassuming 10,000 sq. ft. building on Addison Avenue, west of Harlem. There were always around 100 machines that needed fixing, and the refurbished machines went out the door as fast as the broken ones came in. The warehouse also served as a major meeting place for several of the Outfit's operations.

I invested in two game rooms of my own, one of which was a storefront in a Des Plaines strip mall. We had pinballs, pool tables, a cigarette machine and a soda machine. A smart, sharp-looking, 16-year-old neighborhood kid asked me for a job and I took a liking to him. His parents wanted him to have some responsibility in his life and he brought them in to meet me. Two weeks after I hired him, I was tipped off that he and another kid were going to steal money out of the machines. It didn't make sense that he would do that. I trusted him, I gave him a set of keys, and this is how he was going to repay my trust? I parked my car across the street and, sure enough, they walked in, locked the door, and started emptying the machines. After 10 minutes, I entered the store and locked the door. I said, "Are you guys actually robbing me?" I told the other kid to leave, and relocked the door behind him.

There was some money on my desk and I told my employee to take it, but he wouldn't. I picked him up and threw him on a pool table. Then I slammed a cue stick next to his head so hard that the stick broke in two. The kid pissed his pants and ironically, he did it right next to the *Please Don't Piss on the Pool Tables* sign. I told him to call his parents so he could tell them to come to the store. When they arrived, I had him tell them what he had done and they were extremely grateful that I didn't call the police. Back then, we didn't know that the brains of teenagers weren't fully formed. We just thought they were stupid with incredibly poor judgment.

The only time anyone ever tried to muscle me was when I bought into a well-known home improvement business based on information that Dominic gave me. My partner came into the office one day with a big guy who stood there with his chest puffed up. "This man wants a piece of the business," said my partner. "He's with some people and they want to be partners with us." The other guy was looking at me but didn't say a word. I said to him, "You want a piece of my business?" He answered by saying, "Yeah, we're gonna be your partners." I had to stifle a laugh because he sounded like Fredo Corleone when he told his father he was going to Las Vegas to learn the casino business. "There's people here," I said. "Why don't you guys go over to that restaurant on the corner and I'll be there in five minutes. I gotta finish something up." I wanted a few minutes to think about my response, because, as we all know, first impressions are very important.

When I got there, I saw that the muscle guy was sitting on the inside of the booth, which is where I hoped to find him. I never looked at the big guy. Instead, I sat down across from my partner and kept my eyes glued to his. I didn't think he was in on this but I couldn't let that influence my reaction. I took the fork from my place setting and said to my partner, "I'll tell you what, you tell your friend over here that if he flinches, I'm gonna stick this fork in your neck and then he won't have anybody to run this company, except me. Anybody got anything to say?" I never stopped looking at my partner until I put the fork down and went back to the office. I had probably scared the shit out of my guy, but I was really doing him a favor.

Twenty minutes later the muscle guy came into my office and said, "Jack, I'm sorry, I didn't know who you were. I was trying to make a move. I just called my boss and he told me I had to come back here and apologize." His boss was a good friend of mine and the guy should have done his research before he started freelancing. It's part of the shoot first, ask questions later mentality that a lot of wiseguys used to have.

When I look back on all the things that Dominic Santarelli hooked me up with, I realize that he always sent conmen my way, including this business partner. The guy was likeable enough, but he was a hustler, and the heating business had been his particular hustle for several years. Everybody he hired had to be a hustler, too, and when people are making their living on a commission basis, it can lead to abuses. Hustlers take advantage of people and they prey on senior citizens because they're the most vulnerable and usually the most gullible. I didn't know they were doing it to our customers until the place got raided. Those guys deserved to get caught, and they killed the company in the process. I made decent money, but I never wanted to make money that way.

Almost everyone involved with the company got indicted, including me. At one of the hearings, my partner's attorney told the judge that his client had something to say. I was surprised when my partner told the judge that I had nothing to do with, nor did I have any knowledge of anything he had been doing, and the judge dropped the charges against me. I appreciated what he did because I hadn't asked him to do it. It's nice to know that even hustlers tell the truth at least some of the time, and this time, it was enough to get me off. Nevertheless, another one of my businesses had bitten the dust.

7

THE SHOTS PEOPLE TAKE

I MET MY father at a popular restaurant one night where a lot of wiseguys hung out. I was introduced to a man named Jack McDonald who said he'd like to talk to me. He called me the next day to say he had a very old silver dollar that was worth $200,000, and asked me if I could sell it. "Jack," he said, "the guys who introduced us told me you're a good guy and well liked, so that's why I called you with this." A friend of mine bought and sold rare coins and I told McDonald I'd see what I could do.

My friend looked it up in his book and his glasses almost fell off his face. "Do you know how much this coin is worth," he asked? I nodded, and when I asked him if he could do something with it, he said he was pretty sure he could. I told him to hold on to it and he tried to hand the coin back to me. "I ain't keeping this," he said. I said, "Why not, you're the one with the wall safe. Keep it." About an hour later he walked into my office with a microscope and told me to look at the date on the coin. It was supposed to be from 1804 but I could see that the last number had been a 1, which someone altered to make it look like a 4. You couldn't see that with the naked eye but you couldn't miss it under the microscope.

When McDonald called, I told him I couldn't do anything with the coin. He said he'd come pick it up but I told him I wasn't giving it back. "What do you mean?" he asked. I told him, "It means exactly what I said. Let me ask you something. Why did you decide to make a jagoff out of me? Couldn't you find anybody else? I don't know who the fuck you think I am to put me in this kind of a position, and embarrass me like this, so fuck you!" He said he'd get the coin back and I told him he could try. McDonald went to so many guys that I got several calls and visits from some pretty high-up people. "Look what he did," I told them. "How would you react if someone did this to you? Who the hell would do that? I ain't giving the coin back to him, even though it's worthless." Once I told them what had happened, that was the end of it.

I sent the coin back to McDonald two weeks later. Guys like him never thought about somebody else's reputation because theirs were already ruined. Guys like him think everyone's either stupid or a moron, but fail to recognize those qualities in themselves. It wasn't long before McDonald turned up dead after Tony Accardo found out he was one of the burglars who robbed his house. There's stupid, and then there's really stupid.

Not long after the coin fiasco, a guy called my house and said he needed to talk to me right away. I went to Myron and Phil's restaurant and called him from there. He said, "You have an appointment at nine tomorrow night at Mama Sue's restaurant and you better fucking be there." He was at a motel on Mannheim Road in Rosemont and I told him to wait for me in the coffee shop. When I got there I said, "How long do you know me?" He said, "A long time, Jack." I said, "So where the fuck do you get the nerve to talk to me like that?" He said he was told to tell me that, and I said, "by whom?" When he didn't answer, I got up and walked out to the parking lot. He followed me outside and said, "Jack, you gotta be there." I said, "I don't gotta do anything. You're telling me I have to be there but not who I'm gonna meet. I don't give a fuck who it is. I'm not going, all right?" He said, "Jack, I'm gonna tell you who wants to see you, but you can't tell anyone I told you." He told me it was Turk, a powerful underboss who I knew of, but had never met.

I went to a guy's house, which was something I never did without being invited or calling in advance. He knew Turk, and I told him what was happening. I drove him to the home of the underboss and told him to find out what was going on with this. When he came back to the car, he said, "Don't worry about it. You'll be fine, they just want to hear your side of the story." Based on the location, I knew that someone important was going to show up and, sure enough, in walked Harry Alaman, Butch Petrocelli and Tony Borsolino. I figured I would have been meeting with one of those guys, but I didn't expect to see all three of them.

These guys were the Taylor St. crew, which back then was *the* hit crew in the City of Chicago. Tony was always good to me and so was Harry, but I only knew Butch by reputation. Harry was so hated by the Feds that after he went away, they made sure he spent every holiday season in the Hole so he couldn't have visitors. When Tony got released after serving 13 years, he immediately went back to leading that crew. He was shot to death in 1979 after Butch told the bosses he had lied about something important and the Outfit gave him the go-ahead to whack him. Two years later, the Outfit learned that Butch had lied about Tony, so they had him whacked, too.

Harry and Butch went over to another table and Tony told the guy who instigated this meeting to go sit with them. Tony told me they heard a story that involved me. "Jack," he said, "I just want you to hear me out and then you can tell me your side of it." I told him I knew about this three or four years ago. I said, "Tony, it's bullshit and this guy is a fucking storyteller. He paints pretty pictures for people and he's been doing it his whole life. He once tried to get me to move some valuable old paintings knowing full well they were forgeries. He's full of shit. I hooked this guy up with a couple of lawyers when he came to me with an idea. We laid the whole thing out in Florida before coming back to Chicago. Well, it turned out that the whole thing was a scam. Please tell that guy to come back over here because I want him to hear what I'm about to say."

When the guy came over, I said, "You put me in the middle of this? You told me about this years ago and we looked into it, didn't we? Tony, if there was any money in this it would have been in my pocket a long time ago. He's fucking lying." I looked at the guy and asked him if he had anything to say? He didn't. Tony said, "Nice meeting you, Jack, and thank you for coming." I said, "Tony, please say hello to your wife, Toots, and give her my regards." He looked at me and I said, "Just give her my regards, she's a very nice woman." I know that a guy is automatically going to stick his chest out when somebody brings his wife into the conversation and Tony was probably on the verge of doing that, especially after being locked up for 13 years. I said, "Just take my word for it, Tony," and I left.

A few weeks later my father and I were sitting in the dining room of a steakhouse on Niles Center Road. A waiter walked over and said a guy at the bar wanted to buy me a drink. I looked over and saw Tony Borsolino. His wife used to work downtown while he was in prison. She'd come into my restaurant and order food for her and the girls at her office. I never charged her but I wasn't gonna tell Tony that. Let her tell him that. After Tony found that out about me, I could do no wrong in his eyes. I was just doing the right thing and that's what I've always done. Everybody knew her husband was in the joint, so what was I gonna do, charge her for food?

* * *

Me and a friend of mine were given the exclusive rights to sell scratch-off cards with images of slot machines on them. They came in boxes of 500 and I could sell them wherever I wanted. The cards sold for a buck and people could win anywhere from 50 cents to $200. It cost the locations nothing and that made it a pretty easy sell. All they had to do was collect the money and they got half the take. It was the proverbial gift that kept on giving and everyone was happy except for the Feds, who frowned on these kinds of things.

I put most of the boxes in bars in black neighborhoods and at one point I had almost 50 locations. I'd pull up to places and I could tell that the guys on the corner were wondering what the hell I was doing there. Every couple of weeks I'd pick up the proceeds, give the place their cut, and leave them another box. I always did that by myself and the only other person on the street who knew what I was doing was my partner.

One day, three guys walked into one of the bars and demanded to know whose cards they were. They put such a scare into the owner that he called me. He was still shaking when I got there four hours later. The three guys were from a biker bar across the street and they gave the owner the name of the guy who wanted to talk to me. I walked across the street and was told he was expected at 10 p.m. I came back at 9:45 and there were at least 50 Harleys in the parking lot. A guy named Joe greeted me and we went inside to talk. I said, "Who the fuck are you to walk into that bar like that?" The guy put up his hands and said "Wait, let me get the boss." A guy 20 years older than me, with a huge belly, came in and kept pulling his pants up by the belt loops. "I'm Pepe," he said. "What can I do for you."

I told him I would appreciate it if he didn't interfere with my business. He got right to the point and asked, "You got permission for these things?" I told him I did and he said, "Kid, you better have permission!" He looked like he wanted to eat me and I think he expected me to fold up at the sound of his voice. Instead, I calmly said, "Well, I do, but in this day and age to walk into a bar three strong and scare the shit out of a guy ain't right." I always showed respect to older guys and I said what I needed to say as nicely as I possibly could. He walked me out to my car and said, "I'm gonna be out west tomorrow at 9 a.m. and you better have the okay."

The next day, a friend of mine told me that Pepe had to go on the lam. Ironically, it was my father-in-law who sent him out to California. He was hiding from the police and Frank arranged to keep him somewhere safe for two years. When Pepe went to check me out, my father-in-law found out about it immediately. Later that day he said to me, "I heard you met Pepe," and that was all he said.

Another time, I was introduced to a young woman who was with a guy in his '70s. I didn't know them but they were told they could trust me. The guy would bring me trash bags full of high-end merchandise like Lladro, and I would sell it for them. I'd keep half of whatever I sold and we did this for quite a while. I'd usually give them their money within a week after receiving the merchandise, but I couldn't go anywhere near them because there was some heat on me. I was being followed by the FBI because they were following the car I was driving. That car wasn't mine, but the net effect was the same, and I couldn't take a chance of being stopped with stolen merchandise in my car.

One day a guy called me and said, "Jack, I was told to call you and I was also told to tell you that everything is fine. But you have some merchandise that belongs to somebody and they want it back." I didn't care for that call. I didn't like the implication, but I said I'd bring it to him tomorrow and we set a time and place to meet. I parked two blocks away and left the stuff in the car. I got to the house and saw a mountain of a man standing there. As I was walking up to him, he said, "Jack, just get in your car and follow me."

He went through a couple of alleys and when we stopped, we popped our trunks and I put the bag into his car. The girl was in the car but she didn't get out. The big guy said, "Jack, thanks a lot, I appreciate it." As he started to walk away I said, "Doesn't she want her money?" He walked over to his car and said, "He wants to know if you want your money." She got out of the car, took the money from me without saying a word, got back in the car, and left.

Two years later, I was given some diamonds to fence. The guy brokering the deal was going back and forth with me and I finally said to him, "This is ridiculous. Go tell the people in the other room who I am, and tell them I want to talk to them." The guy went back there and I got invited in. I walked in and Lenny Harris and that mountain of a man were sitting there. Lenny Harris was a top guy in Chicago who ended up getting whacked, and he pointed to mountain man and said, "Remember him?" I said, "I sure do."

"Jack, that girl's partner is a morphine addict and he's nuts," said Lenny. "The fact that you didn't bring the stuff back on time made him worry. He asked her where the money was and why you hadn't brought it to them. She went to the big guy and he came to see me." They called the big guy, Baby Huey, and he was Lenny's muscle. I told Lenny why I was late returning the merchandise and he said, "I knew there had to be a reason, Jack, but the guy wanted to whack you." I said, "Why didn't you just tell me," and he said, "Isn't it better that it worked out this way?"

8
MEMPHIS

IF I COULD change one thing in my life, I would have never gone to Memphis. Some of the situations I've found myself in could have come straight out of a movie. What happened to me at the Memphis International Airport in 1977 is one of them.

Dominic recommended I invest with him in *Casino Records,* a well-known Memphis recording studio. He said we could make a ton of money so I put up $10,000. I knew that *Cadillac Records* had made a fortune in Chicago for its owners and that the Genovese family in New York had made millions of dollars in royalties from their *Roulette* label. The music industry was capable of producing incredible profits and ten thousand dollars could have earned tens of thousands of dollars over time.

Several months later, Dominic called to tell me that a guy named Sam Cammarata was muscling *Casino's* president, Carl Friend, in an attempt to take over the company. Dominic had recently undergone life-saving heart surgery, thanks to me, and asked me if I would check out the situation. I didn't know what was going on, but it sounded like I needed to protect my investment. Carl told me what Sam looked like and when he was coming to Memphis. I flew there to reason with him and to inform him that neither he nor anyone else was going to take the company from us.

I introduced myself to Mr. Cammarata and told him I was an

investor in *Casino Records*. We sat down at the crowded coffee shop and I said, "I'd like you to explain to me what you're attempting to do here." I could see this was a conversation he didn't want to have. As we were getting up to leave, he looked at me and said, "You know what, Jack, fuck you and fuck your Chicago friends, too." I never let anyone talk to me like that, so I said, "No Sam, fuck you!" and punched him as hard as I could. He was unconscious before he hit the floor and I turned and headed down the concourse.

Meanwhile, back on the floor, Sam came out of his coma, pulled a loaded revolver out of his briefcase, and went gunning for me. I just happened to look behind me and saw him sprinting at me with a pistol in his hand. I ran toward the nearest escalator, which was coming up, and I ran down it as fast as I could. Cammarata leaned over the railing and fired two shots at me, one of which ricocheted off the side of the escalator and grazed the elbow of a pregnant Missouri woman. Fortunately for everyone, a very brave security guard tackled Cammarata and prevented him from getting off any more shots.

Seconds later, I was arrested in the parking lot and handcuffed behind my back. All of a sudden, there were security guards everywhere. They took me to a room where a uniformed Memphis police officer guarded me with a shotgun. A second cop showed up a few minutes later and proclaimed, in his heavy southern drawl, "This is the biggest thing that ever hit Memphis." I thought to myself, "Isn't this where Martin Luther King Jr. got killed?"

At that point, two FBI agents walked in. I wondered why they were there, and how they got there so quickly. I started laughing because the whole thing was a joke. I punched a guy, so what? "Go ahead and laugh, Jack," said one of the agents. "We know who you are, and we know you work for Dominic Santarelli." The agent's only question was, "What do you want to tell us?" I looked at them and said, "I don't have anything to say to you, gentlemen." I had been running for my life less than 10 minutes earlier but the FBI wanted me to tell *them* something. They didn't ask me a single question about the incident because they had their own agenda, as did Cammarata. I was trying to push the reset button on my nervous system, because fearing for your life really does a number on you. The way I saw it, if anyone should have been asking the questions, it was me.

There must have been 20 reporters and broadcasters waiting to question me as I walked out of the terminal to a police car. The same people and a few more were at the police station as they walked me in. This was the kind of story that small-town media loved. A Memphis detective escorted me into an interrogation room and asked me if I had anything to say. I told him no and just then, two more FBI agents walked in and told me that I needed to talk to them, which I refused to do. They had no interest in talking about the fact that two shots had been fired at me in a very crowded airport, and that the shooter had tried to kill me. They just wanted me to talk about Dominic Santarelli. The Memphis police department charged me with assault and battery and set my bond at $250, which I had in my pocket.

Dominic and I were still friends, but it was a social relationship after he moved to Ft. Lauderdale on a permanent basis in 1970. When Dominic lived in Chicago, I was single and his marriage was on the rocks. Now our lives were headed in different directions because my wife was expecting our first child around the time that his divorce became final. I saw Dominic two or three times a year, and we spoke on the phone a few times a month. Did I know what he was doing in Ft. Lauderdale? Yes, I did, but only up to a point. Did I care? No. It wasn't any of my business.

Dominic opened Nick's, an Italian restaurant which quickly became the hottest place on Galt Ocean Mile. The Dominic Santarelli that Ft. Lauderdale got to see at Nick's was a charming, outgoing restaurant owner who people loved being around. That was the guy I knew in Chicago, or rather the guy I thought I knew. When I did see Dominic, we had a ball. There were fantastic nightclubs in and around Ft. Lauderdale in the mid-1970s and they all had champagne rooms which were by invitation only. These were the places where the hipper men and sharp women went, and that's what I was doing after my wife and I separated. I'm sure there were agents watching Dominic, which means they could have seen me with him quite a few times.

Apart from my small investment in *Casino Records*, I hadn't been involved in anything with Dominic since he moved to Ft. Lauderdale. I never asked him what he was doing and he never told me. It doesn't matter to me what a man does for a living, you understand, but back then, most people thought Dominic Santarelli was my boss, and I was fine with that. The FBI thought I was Dominic's man in Chicago, and I was fine with that, too. I'll tell you why, but first I need to tell you why I shouldn't have been fine with any of it.

I only recently learned just how dangerous Dominic had become at the time of my 1977 arrest. He had the polish and class to do big things in a legitimate way, but he chose to be a gangster. He went nuts in his pursuit of money and power and he used his power to get more money and power. He became a kind of Dr. Jekyll and Mr. Hyde and the things he got involved in drew the attention of every federal law enforcement agency in the country. He was radioactive and I didn't know it.

Dominic had put some money on the street in Chicago, and he did the same thing in Ft. Lauderdale. I knew that, but I didn't know he immediately built a huge loan-sharking operation. One of the guys who put Dominic's money on the street was Michael Abbate, a guy I met on one of my early trips to Ft. Lauderdale. I didn't care for him and I told Dominic I thought he was a rat. Dominic didn't seem to care and I found that odd, because the deeper in debt guys got, the more likely they were to flip. Flipping is kryptonite to a loan shark and I was pretty sure Abbate would turn on Dominic at some point.

Abbate had borrowed $350,000 in a series of loans over a four-year period, and the weekly interest payments, or vig, were killing him. He went to Dominic's home to make a payment and to rene-gotiate the terms of his loans. According to the affidavit of an ATF agent, Dominic told Abbate that he had killed five men who didn't pay back their loans, and showed him an assortment of firearms which were used in their murders. He also produced a wallet, gold ring and gold wristwatch which Abbate recognized as belonging to one of Dominic's collectors, whose body had recently been found in a parking lot with two bullets in his head.

Less than a month later, Dominic ordered Abbate to take out a $100,000 life insurance policy, with Abbate's wife as beneficiary. Dominic had her sign the policy over to him, just as he had done with two other life insurance policies totalling $150,000. Once Abbate realized he was worth more dead than alive to Dominic, he turned on him and let the FBI wiretap his phone conversations. The information from one of those conversations got the FBI a warrant to search Santarelli's house, during which they carted off eight large cardboard boxes with financial documents and other incriminating items. Many of his loansharking records consisted of notes on index cards and calendars, and slips of paper scattered about his bedroom.

It took five years for a grand jury to return an eight-count indictment against Dominic for conspiracy to commit extortion and income tax evasion. He fled to the Dominican Republic, but was expelled a year later and taken into custody after landing at Miami International Airport. Dominic finally went on trial six years after the FBI's raid on his house and was acquitted of everything but two counts of tax evasion, for which he was sentenced to four years in prison.

In the middle of that loan-sharking investigation, a couple of Americans approached Dominic for help. Robert Wilson and Rich-ard Williams had organized an illegal tax shelter for U.S. citizens through a bank they established in the Bahamas. They lacked the money and connections to get their scheme off the ground, but with Dominic's help, their illegal tax shelter defrauded the U.S.

government out of $140 million dollars in phony tax deductions for 2,000 American citizens, and yielded $17 million in ill-gotten-gains.

Then Williams and Wilson got a little carried away with themselves and asked one of Dominic's contacts to help them establish a national lottery in the Bahamas. Dominic got angry when he learned of that, but it created an opportunity for him to make more money. As punishment for going around him, and the humiliation he said it caused him, Dominic told the two men he was taking a third of their bank. Williams began to argue, at which point Wilson took him into the next room and said, "Look, they were there when we wanted them. I got my money when I needed it. They helped us with the people that we needed in Nassau, set up the trust company, and everything else. Let me work it out." Williams thought a third of the bank was way too much, but Wilson knew they had no choice but to capitulate. "Well," he said, "I don't know about you, but I got kids and I don't intend to argue. You don't argue with people like this. If they say they want a third, they're going to take a third and what the hell are you going to do about it?" Wilson and Williams returned to the room and agreed to Dominic's terms. It was the smart move. Wilson was always smarter.

Wilson and Williams flipped on Dominic, too. He was eventually convicted of extorting more than two million dollars from the tax shelter and for failing to pay taxes on the earnings, and was sentenced to 17 years in prison. I learned about these cases a couple of years ago, and I realized that Dominic was involved in both of those criminal enterprises at the same time he asked me to meet with Cammarata in Memphis. When I said I was fine if the FBI thought I worked for Dominic Santarelli, I had no idea he was involved in any of this. I was just happy they didn't know who I was really with in Chicago.

Few people knew I was aligned with some of the most powerful individuals in the country. For a 33-year-old to be keeping that kind of company was almost unheard of and it would have been stupid to brag about it. What the Feds don't know about you can't hurt you, which is why I kept this a secret. I was about to learn that what the Feds think they know about you, can hurt you more than you can imagine. That, in a nutshell, is the story of my adult life.

I didn't know that Carl Friend had been indicted for fraud after bilking several investors in a scheme involving a Bicentennial record album. I also didn't know that *Casino Records* had paid Dominic $200,000 of the investors money. Cammarata had come to Memphis to give testimony against Carl, and asked the FBI for protection because Dominic had threatened to kill him. I didn't know about that either, and I don't know what Dominic thought would happen by my going to Memphis. It may have been a diversionary tactic to buy him more time to deal with the situation, and if it was, he accomplished that at my everlasting expense.

Lo and behold, it turned out that those first two FBI agents were supposed to meet Cammarata when he deplaned in Memphis because he was in the Witness Protection Program. Had they been on time, this "one-gun-shootout" would have never taken place. I wouldn't have been able to get close enough to Cammarata to have a conversation, much less an altercation, if they had been on time.

Cammarata was charged with attempted murder and assault. He wouldn't have been able to avoid prison time, particularly since he put the lives of dozens of people at risk by shooting at me inside an international airport. Letting Cammarata go on trial would have been a huge embarrassment for the bureau. The FBI would have had to accept responsibility for what their CI did, and for what their agents failed to do. That was never going to happen, because when the Feds screw up, their fallback position is to blame someone else, which in this case was me.

Within an hour, every Memphis media outlet was describing me as "the ballsiest hitman in the country." The evening news shows called it the "Mafia Shootout at Memphis International Airport," even though Cammarata had the only gun. Let's review. Cammarata ran after me, leaned over the second floor railing and fired two shots at me as I was running down the up escalator, unarmed, and in fear for my life. I was running away from the situation, I didn't have a weapon, and who the hell said anything about me wanting to kill him? The Chicago media reported the story the same way, as if the media and the FBI were working in consort in two different cities.

If I had known who Sam Cammarata was, I wouldn't have stepped foot in Memphis. He was a Houston nightclub owner and talent agent who had killed six people by the time he became an FBI informant in 1976. He had connections in Mexico, Colombia and Lebanon, and conspired to kill Lebanon's president, thinking his drug business there would fare much better under a new regime, or so I read. (Six years later, Cammarata was sentenced to 45 years in prison after being convicted of racketeering and drug conspiracy.)

I flew back to Chicago that night and went up the same escalator that I ran down when Cammarata fired at me. There were two large holes no more than four feet apart, and the more I thought about it, the angrier I got. The Dominic I knew in Chicago would have never put me in a situation like that, but this wasn't the same guy. He never said a word to me about what happened that day and he never said anything about the $10,000 I gave him either. I was chasing my money when I went to Memphis and Dominic knew full well that I would. People are always chasing money or sex, or both, but in this case, I wasn't just chasing 10 grand, I was chasing six figures.

The incident was front page news for a week and the local television stations played it up even longer. When I returned for my court date, the district attorney dropped the charges at the request of the FBI. The local media never investigated the incident and the Bureau wasn't held accountable for their screw-up. I would have thought there would have been at least one or two journalists in Memphis who might have questioned the FBI's story because of the obvious holes in it, but nobody did. Most reporters used to believe anything the FBI told them, so if the FBI said it was a shootout, then that's what it was. It's always what the Feds say it is.

The FBI's actions were unethical, immoral and downright cruel, and that's just for starters. They had their own agenda and getting me to flip on Dominic was high on their list. I was charged with assault and battery, but my FBI file said I was charged with Suspicion of Attempted Murder! Who the fuck do these people think they are? The FBI agents flat out lied, and they saddled me with a lifelong reputation as a hitman to cover up their own mistake. From that day forward, every federal agent in the country thought that's what I was. I didn't deserve that treatment, and it hurt my family as much as it hurt me. Soon after Memphis, my daughter told me that a couple of her friends said they couldn't be around her anymore, because I was her father. The Feds call that collateral damage. I call it premeditated slander.

In the late 1980's, my parole officer walked into my Pompano Beach hot dog stand and said he wanted to talk to me. I invited him to sit down and offered him a Chicago-style dog, but he declined. I think he was expecting me to offer him fries, too. "Jack," he said, "you went to Memphis to hit that guy, didn't you?" I said, "Yeah, I hit him and I knocked him out." He said "You're full of shit," and left. The Feds had talked themselves into believing I was one of Dominic's soldiers, and they still thought that way a decade later. In truth, Dominic and I spoke just once more after Memphis, and it was that conversation which put me in the situation that ruined my life.

9

THE FALL OF SPAIN

IN THE HIERARCHY of organized crime, Hyman "Red" Larner was on the same level as his good friend, Meyer Lansky. They were two of the 10 most powerful figures in the country, and the two most powerful ones outside of it. Larner ran all of the Outfit's international gambling operations, except for Cuba, and always made money for his partners, much of which was laundered through his headquarters in Panama. He dealt directly with Manuel Noriega and the Shah of Iran, who he later gave sanctuary to on an island he owned, or so I read. The CIA occasionally worked with Larner, but they never interfered in any of his activities.

Red was a genius and a true visionary. In the early 1970s, he recognized that Spain could become the gambling capital of Europe and he bided his time until its longtime dictator, Generalissimo Francisco Franco died. Spain soon legalized casino gambling, and Red negotiated a deal with the leaders of the country's emerging democracy to let Chicago set up and run the casinos. This I know.

Mr. Larner believed that Spain would create more revenue for Chicago than Las Vegas ever did. He was getting up in age and he told the Outfit they needed to select the right person to get their operation up and running. They sought out the candidates, rather than the other way around. In the world of organized crime, respect filtered up, meaning it had to be earned before it was bestowed. A shortlist of capable guys was put together from which they would make their selection, and just having your name on that list was a major accomplishment. The Outfit kept things so close to the vest that nobody on their list knew they were being evaluated for that position, or that the position even existed.

I hadn't heard of Mr. Larner until I was introduced to him in 1977 by one of my good friends, who, unbeknownst to me, was Red's eyes and ears and one of his most trusted lieutenants. Red started taking me to people's homes for cocktail parties and informal get-togethers. He introduced me to everyone, but the only name that was ever mentioned was mine. I didn't know who the people were or why I was there, but everyone was well dressed, well spoken and smart. I had been invited into an exclusive world where a lot of people could meet me in a relaxed, social setting.

The oldtimers used to operate like a Board of Directors made up entirely of CEOs. They sat back and waited for somebody to say something negative or positive about me and it was all very low key. By constantly putting me with new people, Red was able to draw upon a lot of first impressions from people he knew and respected. The Outfit was only going to get one shot at this, so they couldn't afford it to screw it up. The hiring decision was Red's to make, but all the top guys had to sign off on it, including Tony Accardo.

In early 1978, I drove my friend to his home. As he got out of the car, he said, "Pick me up at 11 tomorrow. We're gonna have lunch at Jack's restaurant in Lincolnwood." That's all he said. When we got to Jack's the following day, I saw Mr. Larner sitting at a table and his driver waved us over. We talked about normal, everyday things over lunch, after which Mr. Larner said, "Jack, take a walk with me." He and I walked along Touhy Avenue when he informed me that Spain recently legalized casino gambling, and that I had been chosen to run the operation for the Outfit. "We'll get into the particulars later," he said, "but be prepared to go to Spain relatively soon." I was too stunned to speak, and he looked at me and said, "Don't worry. Everything will be fine."

The Outfit could have chosen anybody in the world to build their gambling operation in Spain, and they chose me, Jack Louis Gail. I felt like I was being made. I was hired on the basis of my character, reputation and track record and my resume was a matter of public record. I told my father the news and he paid me the best compliment of my life. "You used to be Lenny Gail's son," he said. "Now I'm Jack Gail's father."

A couple of months later, my friend and I were on a flight to Spain. I couldn't tell anyone where I was going, so I basically disappeared for about six weeks. We based ourselves at a five-star hotel in Madrid and met with Mr. Larner almost every day for a month, scouting potential properties for our casinos. I've had a lot of great ideas in my life, but the one I came up with in Spain was by far the best.

We'd be working off a clean slate, and my idea involved much more than just gambling and the revenue from it. The first step was to purchase 800 acres of land within driving distance of many of Spain's metropolitan areas. The property would be anchored by a 2.5 mile, Nascar-inspired track. That's the size of the Indianapolis Motor Speedway oval, only this would be an amusement park ride. Full-size Nascars on monorails, three abreast, would duplicate the racing experience on the safest form of transportation in the world. Kids from 9 to 90 would get to feel what it's like to drive in excess of 200 miles per hour, two people to a car, complete with the sounds of what an actual driver would hear and directions on when to shift. They wouldn't be driving the vehicle but it would feel like they were. It would take less than 60 seconds to circle that 2.5 mile track, once the car was fully powered. I anticipated a 20-minute ride, unlike the two-and-a-half minute rides I grew up with at Riverview Amusement Park in Chicago.

Inside the park would be 300 acres of land, of which 200 were buildable. For perspective, 200 acres is the size of the original Las

Vegas Strip. In other words, it's huge. I planned to erect the most amazing theme park the world had ever seen. I'd fill it with the best roller coasters, a large outdoor concert venue, an indoor shopping mall and plenty of food courts. There'd be two giant ferris wheels from which you could watch Nascar vehicles silently circling the track at speeds that would take your breath away just by watching them. My plan included a water park and a petting zoo for children, with plenty of clean, well-maintained restrooms throughout the entire facility. Outside the park would be a campground, an RV park, a Harley bar and rest area, and two hela-pads. There'd be something for everyone, and people could vacation in style at any of three casinos that would be owned and operated by the largest hotel chains in Europe. We're talking Crown Jewel property here.

This would have been the biggest thing the Outfit ever had in one spot, and it carried with it very little risk. We wouldn't own anything on the property unless we decided to put a small casino of our own inside the park. That aside, all we'd own was the very valuable property on which everything sat. The income from our long-term, percentage-based leases would produce a fortune, year in and year out, and everything about it was legitimate. Mob, shmob. We were American businessmen who were looking to create a destination that would have attracted tourists from all over the world and generated huge tax revenue for the people of Spain.

The idea was genius, and Red recognized it right away. After he read my three-page, hand written proposal, he looked at me and said, "How did you come up with a concept like this? This is phenomenal. We could do this, Jack." That's how we left it, and a few days later I came back to Chicago to get my affairs in order. I was sitting on top of the world, but my world was about to get rocked.

10

STUPID IS AS STUPID DOES

THE LAST FAVOR Dominic Santarelli asked me to do for him made no sense. He had no business asking me to do it, and I had no business doing it. It involved weapons and he knew I never had anything to do with weapons or drugs. Dominic told me that a guy named Frank Ammirato needed two silencers to send out of the country and he asked me to get them for him. I had a bad feeling about it because there's no legal use for silencers, but I ignored my gut and my brain. Well, stupid is as stupid does when you're loyal to the wrong person. I made a couple of calls, got the silencers, and made sure that nobody saw me give them to Ammirato. I didn't gain financially from the transaction, nor was I reimbursed for my out-of-pocket costs. I thought that was the end of it, but that small favor landed me in the middle of two criminal conspiracies which put me in federal prison for four-and-a-half years. And if that weren't bad enough, the arrest came back to haunt me 13 years later and bit my ass even harder.

My one-time best friend ended up betraying me, the one person I thought he would never betray. Dominic was incapable of being loyal to anyone, and I learned it the hard way. He cost me my reputation and a hell of a lot more. I spent 15 years in prison because of his betrayal. I got ruined financially because of him; I lost my opportunity to run the Outfit's gambling operations and interests in Spain because of him; and I lost the love of my life because of him. But when my ex-wife and my fiance called Dominic for help in getting me out of a situation that he willfully and cunningly put me into, he laughed at both of them and hung up the phone.

Of course, that means he laughed at me, too. He laughed at the thought of helping his most valued friend, the same friend who saved his life two years earlier. Given what he did to me, most people would have understood if I had informed on him. Well, I must either be the most loyal person in the universe, the stupidest, or both, because my blind loyalty prevailed over reason, self-preservation and what my gut was telling me. The Feds always assumed I would turn on Dominic, and when I chose to do my time, they never forgave me. Back then, not flipping was considered to be a crime to most agents, several of whom made it a priority to punish me for that so-called crime if they ever got another chance.

I didn't know that Ammirato was doing major deals with three guys who were actually wired-up federal agents. For reasons I will never know, Ammirato described me as a major mob figure in his conversations with the agents. I had lunch one day with Frank at a restaurant on Mannheim Rd. during which those three agents joined us. I didn't care for them, and I had no reason to believe I'd ever see them again.

Two weeks before I was to move to Spain, the three undercover agents called and said they wanted to meet with me over dinner. There was no reason why I should have gone, because my involvement in their deal, such as it was, was over, but I went. We left the restaurant and in the middle of the parking lot, one of them said, "Jack, you're under arrest. We're ATF agents." At that point, three more agents joined us. They were all gentlemen and they didn't draw their guns or act like tough guys, nor did I. I was taken to the Federal Building where ATF special agent James Delorto gave me several reasons why I should cooperate with them. "We know you didn't hurt anybody," said Delorto. "We just want you to flip on

Santarelli." When I refused to turn on anyone, they drove me to the Metropolitan Correctional Center (MCC) for booking.

Two weeks later, three buses took me and 50 other inmates to the Marshal's lockup at the Federal Building. The lockup is a large cell where they put everyone before their court appearances and I was one of the first to be taken to the courtroom. A couple of minutes into the proceedings, an Assistant U.S. Attorney by the name of Gary Shapiro claimed I had probably killed Sam Giancana. The courtroom fell silent and everybody looked at him. The judge put his hands on his desk and stood up very slowly. "Mr. Shapiro," he said, "are you accusing Mr. Gail of that crime?" Shapiro said, "Well, no, not exactly." The judge told him to sit down and remain silent for the duration of the hearing. Within five minutes, my bail was set and they took me back to lockup.

By the end of the day, everyone but me was put back on the bus. I knew something was up and sure enough, agent Delorto walked in and said, "Guess what, Jack? All the buses are gone. I need to walk you back to the MCC." I've never heard of an agent walking a defendant back to jail and I don't think I've ever even seen that in a movie, either. Delorto wanted a chance to talk to me alone and that was how he did it. He didn't handcuff me, but he had his service revolver and there were at least two or three more agents on foot or in an unmarked vehicle in the event I suddenly turned stupid and tried to escape. Of course, it's hard to get lost in a crowd when you're the only one wearing an orange jumpsuit.

Delorto knew that Santarelli had put me into this jackpot and he figured that was reason enough for me to turn on him. Delorto wouldn't take no for an answer, ever! From the moment the Feds arrested me, they wanted me to flip on Dominic. Delorto flat out told me, "Rat on Santarelli and we can make this go away." He knew how limited my involvement was and appeared to be shocked when I declined what he thought was a very generous offer.

By this time, every lawyer in Chicago thought I was a straight up hitman. After my arrest, I got shunned by a lot of people I used to know. Once you become a felon in this country, you're automatically a liar, as if by definition. Your previous reputation means nothing because most people believe you are what the Feds say you are. The people who used to come to me for favors couldn't get away from me fast enough, and I've never been able to overcome it.

When I didn't give Dominic up, I did that for my sake, rather than his. I found it ridiculous that the federal government thought I would let them take my soul. That I cannot do, and I will give you my reason. I wanted my children to be able to walk down the street without having people say, "There goes that rat motherfucker's kids." That's what people say behind your back, but they weren't going to be able to say that about me.

The Feds demonstrated just how power hungry they were by setting my bail at half a million cash. I had gotten somebody two silencers which were never used, and I hadn't even met five of the other six guys in this misguided caper. Nevertheless, my bail was larger than what many accused murderers get. They were sending me a not-so-subtle message that I was going to flip on Dominic Santarelli, come hell or high water.

We managed to get the bail lowered to $75,000 and my father put his house up as collateral. At one point, he said, "What the fuck do we do?" I told him I was thinking about skipping bail, and without missing a beat, he said, "Well, if I'm gonna lose my house, I'm going with you." That was my father's sense of humor. He taught me something that Jews have known for thousands of years; when things get real bad, you have to laugh. God should have made that his Eleventh Commandment. Trust No One should have been his Twelfth.

The trial for the other six guys began on May 21, 1979. Ammi-rato was the ringleader and had the most to gain by flipping on Dominic. He chose not to, but it was the way he did it that got my attention. He waived his right to a trial and told the court he wanted to change his plea from not guilty to guilty on all counts. Questioned by the judge, Frank assured the court that he did so because he was in fact guilty, and not because he had been threatened or promised anything by anyone. The judge reminded Ammirato he was facing a possible 243 years in prison, but he didn't seem to care. He ended up getting 26 years, as did all but one of the other co-conspirators. That's half a lifetime to some guys, but not one of them flipped.

I was the only defendant who fought the charges, but any chance of my beating the rap was gone after what Ammirato told the undercover agents about me. The things that came out of Frank's mouth were absolutely ludicrous. A couple of years prior to my arrest, there had been a drug deal in Ft. Lauderdale involving a million dollars in cocaine and a million dollars in cash. Ammirato told the Feds that I had masterminded the job, and that it was far from the biggest heist my crew and I ever pulled. Just because someone says something about you doesn't make it true, but the prosecution claimed I was capable of that and much, much more. They thought too much of me. I'm not that clever. The Feds case was more about what they thought I was doing than what I had done. And, as you may know, people will believe what they want to believe, especially if it confirms that which they already think is true.

Frank's operation had nothing to do with me but that didn't stop the ATF from shoving it up my tuchis. After the incident in Memphis, the FBI joined forces with the ATF to get Dominic. They made their move relatively quickly on Ammirato, and his stupidity brought them to me. The ATF infiltrated his operation thinking they would get to Dominic but nobody flipped on him. The only reason they came at me was because the FBI described me as a hitman after the incident in Memphis. It was a lie but it was all the Feds needed to put me on their radar.

Most of the counts in the indictments were prefaced with the words conspiring, distributing, possessing, transferring, shipping, delivering or engaging, and all of them concerned weapons and drugs. The agents testified they were looking for somebody to sell them marijuana, quaaludes and cocaine. Anytime drugs or weapons were mentioned during a taped conversation, the prosecutor made them into separate crimes, even if the agents were the only ones who talked about it. The prosecutors brought up Cosa Nostra and claimed I had been closely involved with Sam Giancana, without presenting any evidence to support their claim. My only involvement in this operation was procuring two silencers, but it didn't matter. The Feds think that one crime leads to another, which leads to another, et cetera, et cetera. The stories that Ammirato told the Feds were all they needed to justify their pursuit of me.

My attorney had no idea what was going on. I asked him why he wasn't challenging anything the prosecution was saying about me, and he said, "I don't want to piss off the judge." I said, "What do you mean you don't want to piss him off? He's mad at me already." Everyone knows you don't stand a chance in court if you're too poor to hire your own attorney. If you hire an incompetent attorney, you don't stand a chance, either, even if you paid him $50,000 like I did. When my attorney finally started objecting, he kept getting over-ruled. After his fourth objection, I pulled on one of his belt loops and told him to sit down. Sure enough, I was convicted of crimes that I did not commit, in addition to the one that I did. Two and a half months after being convicted, I was sentenced to 14 years in federal prison. I didn't get 14 years for trafficking in drugs or weapons. I got 14 years for not cooperating with the Feds and not turning on Dominic Santarelli.

After my indictment, I never spoke with Dominic again. He avoided prison until 1985 and died of a heart attack 10 years later, shortly before he was to be released. Ironically, the last 19 years of Dominic's life were a gift from me. He suffered a major heart attack in Ft. Lauderdale and needed bypass surgery, which in the mid-1970's, was not a routine operation. The Cleveland Clinic had the best cardiac unit in the country, but they also had a six-month waiting list. Dom asked me for help and I turned to Joe Kellman, whose family had contributed millions of dollars to the Clinic. When I told them Dominic was one of my best friends and that he might not survive the wait, the family got him moved to the front of the surgical list. Two weeks later he had the procedure. That favor wasn't a big deal to me because if you don't do something when you can, what the hell good are you? I guess Dominic didn't consider it a big deal either, because he never thanked me for saving his goddamn life.

People can be taken in by certain kinds of individuals, like I was by Dominic Santarelli. I was seduced by the ride he took me on and other than being with my second wife, I never enjoyed life more. Back then, I had no reason to think Dominic was anyone other than who I thought he was, and I never looked for signs that might have indicated otherwise. By the time I discovered his true self, it was too late to do anything about it. After everything I had done for him, he conned me, and I still can't figure out why. I should have seen it coming, but I didn't. Let me give you a piece of advice. You need to question your assumptions every so often, especially those that you take for granted, like who your real friends are.

11

FROM HEAVEN TO HELL

MY HEAD DIDN'T come out of the ether for a long time. I finally realized that if I didn't get my mind off the street, it would drive me insane. That meant I had to do the time, and not let the time do me. It's the only way to keep your sanity in prison, but not everyone can do it. Back then, the sentencing guidelines were such that I knew I'd serve no more than five years, but five years is a long time to spend behind bars.

I put every person I knew in an imaginary circle and analyzed my relationship with all of them. Those who had a role in causing my incarceration were the first to leave the circle. Then I identified the people of questionable or inconsistent character, and they too were banished. Most of the people I knew in Florida were cut loose, as were the guys who I only saw when they needed something. At the end of the process, I realized I didn't have nearly as many friends as I thought I had, and wondered how I could have spent so much time around so many ignorant people.

I lost Bonnie Sharkey because of this, and that was the unkindest cut of all. I met Bonnie in Cleveland at the wedding of the daughter of a friend of Dominic's and mine. We were with the groom when I was hit with the thunderbolt. I locked eyes with the most beautiful woman I had ever seen as she walked across the room, as if in slow motion. The groom told me she was his cousin, Bonita. I asked him if she was married and he said no. "Well then,' I said, "is she with anybody?" He said, "kinda, sorta." Kinda, sorta? I laughed and said, "Go get her!"

He walked Bonnie over and we introduced ourselves. Dominic was trying to be suave and I looked at him and said, "Forget about it, you ain't got a shot." Bonnie and I walked over to the bar and we just kept on talking to each other. Some of her family and friends came over and it wound up being a very nice evening. The next day she brought her best friend to meet me and we had brunch. When she drove me to the airport the following morning, I asked her if she wanted to come to Chicago, and she said yes.

Bonnie grew up surrounded by mob guys because her father was in the concrete business and the mob was in the construction business. Like my father, Ray Sharkey was respected by everyone. Outfit guys always wanted to be around professional Italian fighters, which Ray had been, and they enjoyed great and enduring relationships, not just in Cleveland or Chicago, but all across the country.

One of Ray's best friends was John Scalish, the boss of Cleveland's Mayfield Mob for 32 years. Made guys came to the Sharkey's house in Cleveland, but Scalish only came to their place on Put-In-Bay, a one-by-three-mile island accessible only by boat, ferry or plane. It was one of the few places where he could actually relax. Ray bought a new bed and installed Italian tile in the master bathroom which was John's room whenever he wanted it. He used to let Bonnie's sisters drive his car around the island and gave them candy.

Being as gorgeous as Bonnie was, every guy and his brother hit on her but she was able to deflect most of their attention. Once she and I hooked up, everybody knew she was with 'Jack from Chicago,' and nobody messed around with her after that. Bonnie wanted the kind of legitimate relationship that most wiseguys either wouldn't or couldn't give her, and potential suitors never pressured her like they pressured other women, because Bonnie wasn't like other women. I've always thought of her as a female version of me.

Bonnie took me to Put-in-Bay to meet her parents, and her father made me sleep on the porch. She was 24 when I met her and she moved to Chicago on her 26th birthday. Her parents gave her a combination birthday/going-away party, after which we got in her car and drove all night to Chicago. I moved out of Lake Point Tower and got us an apartment on Lake Shore Drive that overlooked most of Wrigley Field. Bonnie liked how I furnished the place except for the brown and white couch which reminded her of a cow. I was thinking the same thing when I bought it but what kind of a guy makes a fuss over a couch? I know the answer now, but back then I didn't.

And then, it was over. I was arrested three months after Bonnie moved to Chicago. I knew I was going to get ruined and I knew what I had to do. Bonnie was getting ready to go to work when I came home. The lights were off and I kept them off. I told her we had to split up and that she needed to make a life for herself. She had seen my story on the news and in the papers over the previous couple of weeks, but I had avoided talking about it. Bonnie said she'd wait for me - and she would have - but I ignored her. As I walked away, she was crying and calling my name but I kept on walking. I wanted her to hate me, thinking it might make it easier for her to move on with her life.

If you have a woman like Bonnie on the street, it'll drive you insane. I'd heard the stories about what happens to relationships when a guy does time and I saw it for myself after I went to the joint. Guys would call their wives every day. Then they wouldn't talk to them every day or even every week and, at some point, the wives stopped answering the phone. A guy would answer and say, "What do you want?" When he said he wanted to talk to his wife, the guy on the other end of the phone would tell him to fuck off and not call there again. This happened all the time. Some guys walked around like they were going to explode, while others just sat there and cried like babies. "Oh no, my wife. Ah tu madre, what am I gonna do?"

Being in prison is bad enough, but to do your time with that on your mind would be a continuous form of torture. Thanks, but no thanks.

I chased Bonnie out of my life for both of our sakes, but I did it mostly for her. She would have been putting her life on hold for me and you know what I would have been doing if we went that route? I would have wondered what she was doing day and night, even though she's the most loyal woman in the world. That kind of situation is guaranteed to drive you crazy so I tried to spare both of us any more pain and heartache. I'm not the kind of selfish fuck who would make it all about me. I was the one who screwed up, not Bonnie! It was my life being put on hold, not hers! Why should she have to waste years of her life because of me? Pushing Bonnie away was the most painful thing I ever did but I really had no other choice.

Bonnie stayed in Chicago rather than moving back to Cleveland. I heard through the grapevine that she went to the schvitz (steambath) at Sunset Bowl on Western Avenue and asked some of the wiseguys who hung out there to tell her where I was, but no one did. She ended up marrying one of her fellow bartenders two years after I went away. I didn't hear about that because I didn't want to. When Bonnie's mother got cancer, her family was told that she would need at least two full-time caregivers to provide the round-the-clock care in order to keep her at home. Bonnie immediately left her job and her apartment in Chicago to move back to Cleveland. Her youngest sister was living in Florida at the time and she also dropped everything in order to be with Gladys Sharkey for the last seven months of her life. It would have been out of character for Bonnie to do anything else.

12
LIFE INSIDE

I NEVER THOUGHT about prison because I never did anything that would have put me there. Like most people, all I knew about prison was what I saw on television and in the movies. The oldtimers never talked about their experiences behind bars any more than GI's like my father talked about their experiences in the war.

The first chance I got, I called my ex-wife, my kids and my father. You can only call so many people from jail so you make the most important calls first. Life goes on but it goes on without you and you're on your own in every conceivable way. I felt as out of place as Donald Trump at a library. My bedroom was a shared cage and everywhere I looked there were bars and concrete. All I could control was the space around me, and how I reacted to my situation. Getting angry or depressed was not an option.

I got along well with all of the bureaucrats in the prison system and it helped that I made them laugh. Laughter is a scarce commodity in prison and the staff needs it as much as the inmates do. The problem is there's nothing funny about being in prison. Going through life without a sense of humor is bad enough, but being incarcerated without one would be unbearable. So, I tried to amuse myself. One day, I was carrying a towel and I said to a guard, "Excuse me, I'm new here. Can you tell me how to get to the beach?" He wasn't nearly as amused as I was.

Miss Christmas was a unit manager who I met after getting to the MCC. She was a big, beautiful, single, black woman who adopted two white children. She was tough, but fair. A week after I got there, she called me into her office and said: "Mr. Gail, I got along very well with Mr. Carlisi and I got along very well with Mr. Alex, and I know I'm going to get along very well with you." I said, "I would think so, Miss Christmas, and I'm pleased to meet you." Sam Carlisi and Gussie Alex were in the hierarchy of organized crime in Chicago, and I found it stunning that she put me on their level. It was an example of how the reputation that the FBI created for me just kept rolling right along. Once you've been labeled a hitman by federal law enforcement, you're stamped with a reputation that you simply can't get away from, even if the charge is untrue.

I was what they call a Neutron in prison. I had my own back, as it were, and everyone knew I didn't have a bone to pick with anyone. Water seeks its own level, and so do human beings. People hook up with their own kind in prison, and I identified the shot-callers. There's a hierarchy and a structure to things and I really got a kick out of observing that. You'd be walking in from the yard and, bang, somebody would punch somebody over some petty bullshit and two gangs would start fighting. They considered themselves such bad asses that they were always having to prove to themselves just how bad they were.

I had never heard of Thorazine until I got to the MCC. A lot of inmates were in various stages of mental illness and would walk around like zombies in a Thorazine-induced drug stupor. When I first got there, I'd use the phone and this one guy would come and sit and stare at me. After the second time, I asked him if he wanted to make a call but he didn't say a word and I let it go. The next time I used the phone, I saw this guy coming down the stairs, and was about to confront him when another guy walked between us and said, "Jack, don't do it. He's on Thorazine." I was glad he told me because the world's different inside, and the sooner you realize it, the better off you are.

I got to dinner late one night and the guy working the counter hesitated before giving me the tray. He was a black guy, and I looked at him and said, "What?" He said, "Well, you're late." I said, "Who the fuck are you?" There was a cop sitting right there at the desk and I looked at him. Then I put my hand underneath the tray full of food and pushed it into the face of the guy who gave it to me. I told the cop, "Don't move," and he didn't. I looked back at the guy and said, "Fuck you, what are you gonna do, sell it?" The guy walked away, but that didn't mean the situation was over.

A gang member's first reaction is to stick up for one of their own. That could have been a very touchy situation because when you get in a beef with one gang member, you get in a beef with all of them. That's when it pays to be a Neutron. All the gang leaders asked what happened, and when they found out it was me, they let it go. If anything, they respected me more as a result of it, because they equate weakness with cowardice.

A month after being convicted, a guard woke me at 5 a.m. and told me I was going to court. I told him didn't have a court date, but he said I had to go because my name was on the list. They put me on a bus and took me to the marshal's lockup. A jail guard came to the cell door and walked me to where James Delorto and some guards were standing. Delorto told me Assistant U.S. Attorney Mitchell Mars wanted to talk to me. I said, "I don't have to listen to this," and I walked away. "No, Jack," he said, "you got a problem and you need to listen."

Delorto took me to an office on the 14th floor of the courthouse where Mars introduced himself to me and said, "I want you to testify before the grand jury regarding the weapons." I said, "You mean the weapons that I'm doing time for? Well, you're a little late, aren't you?" "No, Jack," he said, "we're not late. Let me inform you that if you refuse to testify we're going to ask the chief judge to hold you in contempt of court."

At that point, my body started to shake, and they could see it.

I said, "Correct me if I'm wrong, but if I refuse to testify, the time I'm doing stops and I have to do the 18-month life of the grand jury which can be extended for an additional 18 months?" He nodded, and at that moment nothing would have given me greater pleasure than to beat the shit out of him. I looked at Mars and said, "Can I use that phone?" He dialed the number of my attorney and handed me the phone. I told him I was in Mitchell Mars' office and that he wanted me to testify before a grand jury. "I'm not going to do it," I said, "so you talk to him." I lobbed the receiver onto his midsection and though it didn't land hard enough to wrinkle his shirt, he seemed quite offended by the gesture.

Anyway, I wouldn't testify and they held me in contempt. My time stopped and I said to myself, "What the hell is this?" I already had to serve a little over four years, and this little putz wanted to add another three years of contempt time unless I flipped. Why did I deserve such generosity? I just wanted to be left alone to do my time.

Seven weeks later, I hired an attorney to get me off the contempt charge. As we walked out of the chambers, I heard Mitchell Mars tell my attorney that all he wanted to know was who else I sold the weapons to. When I heard that, I turned around and said, "If that's what you want to know, let's go back to court right now." My attorney told me to go back to the MCC because he wanted to talk to Mars first.

I went before the Grand Jury two weeks later and I lied, and I'll tell you why I did. They had already given me 14 years for getting someone two silencers which were never used. Everything else they said I did was made up to make me look almost as bad as the real conspirators. I wasn't going to inform on anyone, so I told the grand jury I went to a designated place, popped my trunk, and went to make a phone call. When I returned to my car, the trunk was closed. One of the grand jurors said, "Mr. Gail. Do you expect us to believe this story?" I said, "Personally sir, I don't care what you believe. All I can tell you is what happened that day." The fact that I testified got me off the contempt charge, but if the Feds think you lied to them, they come at you with everything they have. Four months later, I received a letter informing me I was the target of a perjury investigation based on my Grand Jury testimony. It didn't go anywhere, and that apparently pissed them off even more.

The U.S. Attorney's office wanted me to flip on Dominic and a retired Chicago detective with whom I'm still close. If it took the prospect of adding another 18 or 36 months to my prison time to get me to do it, that was fine with them. I've never betrayed anyone in my life but they never stopped trying to change that. The Feds don't give a damn about a person's integrity or principles. They compete among themselves to see how many guys they can get to turn and all I was to them was a potential notch on someone's belt. That kind of behavior may be perfectly normal in their alternative universe but it shouldn't be normal in the one everybody else inhabits.

One day at the MCC, an inmate named John got into an argument with a female officer in the dining room. He was very angry, and when he raised his hand to slap her I stood up and hollered, "John, don't do that." Luckily he stopped and that was the end of it. I asked the officer to please let it go and I thought she did. Instead, I got written up because I involved myself in the situation, a fact which I didn't learn until I was transferred to the federal prison in Milan, Michigan, and my new case manager pulled a letter from my file and read it aloud. Letters that end up in your file are almost always bad and sure enough, the unit manager called me into his office. The letter said I was an influence on a prisoner named John, but it didn't say that I had defused a potentially bad situation. The unit manager didn't know about that and he tore up the letter after I told him what had happened.

The first thing you do when you get to a prison is clean up your area and make your bed. I did that and was walking down the stairs when I heard a guy say, "5-O." I turned around and saw half a dozen black guys under the stairwell. I said, "What did you say?" One guy said "Come on Pops, leave it alone." That bothered me all night so the next morning I went up to one of those guys and said I needed to talk to the guy who had the deck. After he conferred with somebody, he came back and took me to the head guy. I said, "Look, I'm walking down the stairs and this guy says 5-O." "I was there when it happened," he said. "You reminded the guy of a police detective in his district who had hair like yours. That's what he meant." I said, "Well, where I come from, when you call somebody 5-O, you're referring to him as a rat." He said, "Jack, I know who you are. He didn't mean any disrespect with it." I said fine and we laughed about it, and that's how you generate goodwill in prison.

A majority of the people who work in federal prisons are actually decent folks but there's always an asshole with an attitude. The worst employees were women. A lot of them were petty and vindictive and it showed in the way they treated guys. Maybe the reason they did it was because of the abuse they endured from both inmates and male guards. If I were a woman, the prison system is the last place I'd want to work.

The prison would feed inmates unit by unit and 200 guys would eat at the same time. Female guards would usually walk the room and when they passed my table, I'd say, "Why don't you give me the check?" People would look at me like I was out of my cotton-picking mind, so I'd also say, "And give me the check for that table over there, too." I got the feeling that most of the people there had never heard of picking up a check and just didn't want to admit it.

I wanted out of Milan from the day I arrived. I didn't know anyone there and I would have froze my ass off half the year. That's no way to do time, but you can't just request a transfer because the accommodations aren't to your liking.

I devised a scheme which I hoped would get me to a federal prison in Florida. I called my father and asked him to tell my prosecutor that I wanted to talk to him. My father agreed to make the call but only after asking me if I was sure about wanting to do this.

Four days later, two U.S. Marshals escorted me to the back of an airplane for the two-and-a-half hour plane ride to Miami, where I spent the night at the Dade County Jail.

The following morning I was taken to a courtroom where one of the assistant U.S. Attorneys who prosecuted my case was waiting for me with a colleague of his that I hadn't met. "Where do you want to start?" he said. I politely pushed a stack of papers at him and said, "I got sentenced for things I wasn't involved in, and I'd like to point out a lot of false statements in the case that were made against me." Very nonchalantly, he pushed the documents to the side and said, "We'll get into that later. Now where do you want to start." I pushed the papers back in his direction, and said, "This *is* where I want to start." He said, "Wait a minute, your father called and said you wanted to talk to me." I said, "I am talking to you." It almost sounded like a "who's on first" routine, but the prosecutors were anything but amused. They looked at each other and got up and left, leaving me there by myself. I resisted the temptation to find the exit and several minutes later two cops came to take me back to jail.

13

POMP AND CIRCUMSTANTIAL EVIDENCE

I SPENT THE next eight months at Homestead prison in Florida waiting for the other shoe to drop. Did I use the system to my advantage? No question about it. But before you start thinking that I was just being clever, you need to understand the seriousness of what I did, and the courage it took to do it. The prosecutor had flown me to Florida at considerable expense because he expected me to cooperate with him. The Feds approach a conversation like this solely in terms of what you can do for them, and the only thing you can do for them is to inform on other people. The Feds tried to get me to flip before my trial, after my conviction, and after I was sentenced. They always expected me to trade my soul for a get-out-of-jail-early card, because they expect everybody to make that deal.

Everybody had to work at an assigned job at Homestead, and some jobs were a lot better than others. A friend of mine told me I should attend a culinary class. The guy who ran the class wasn't a convict but he liked wiseguys. I interviewed with the guy and he asked me about my expertise in the culinary arts. I responded by saying, "I make the best popcorn you've ever had." He laughed and said, "Your job from now on is to sit right here in front of my desk and make me laugh," which I did for eight months. We ate great food, watched TV, and laughed for three hours each morning, It's good work if you can get it, even at five cents an hour.

My time at Homestead taught me that guys who complain the most, tend to be the weakest. Guys who were tough on the street would come to me and say, "Jack, this guy is bothering me." I'd say, "If he's bothering you, then crack him." Even some of the bosses were weak once they got behind bars. The boss of a major midwestern city was there the same time that I was. I'll call him Vito because I don't want to use his real name. Vito was suspected of ordering the hit on Jimmy Hoffa, and he did something that I wouldn't have expected from a man of his stature. We were in the visiting room and he came up to me and said, "Jackie, do you know this kid?" I looked at the kid and he was cracking up. Vito said, "This motherfucker was in the women's bathroom getting a blow job when my wife went in there. She saw this and was mortified."

My initial thought was how did the kid manage to get in the women's bathroom in the first place? Vito wanted me to punish the kid. I said, "Vito, you want me to crack him? For what?" He said, "My wife can't even go into this bathroom over here. What kinda shit is this?" I said, "Vito, do you know how long this kid's been down?" He said, "What's that got to do with it?" The fact was that most guys in the joint would have killed to get a blow job so I told him, "If you want him cracked, you crack him. I ain't crackin' anybody over a blow job."

What I didn't tell him was that if he grabbed that kid, the kid would have killed him on the spot because he didn't give a fuck about anything. Vito was a moron for even bringing it up and he should have told his wife to stop talking and leave it alone. What right did she have to be upset about that, or about anything for that matter? She was visiting a prison, for Christ's sake, not a summer camp for kids.

Well, all good things must end, including my time in Florida. When I wouldn't flip, the prosecutor felt like I had betrayed him. He punished me by putting me on a two-and-a-half month bus tour back to Milan, Michigan. They call it "diesel therapy," and I spent time in five different joints along the way. I was in the Hole for five days at the first stop, after which they shipped me to Atlanta where I spent another five days in the Hole. This was July and August, and everybody was walking around in their underwear. There's only so much that prosecutors can do to get back at you, and diesel therapy is one of their favorite weapons.

It was business as usual when I returned to Milan. When guys asked me what happened, I told them it took me two-and-a-half hours to get there and two-and-a-half months to get back. There wasn't one guy in the joint who didn't laugh or curse when he heard that line. The Feds would periodically visit and show me pictures of wiseguys on whom they wanted me to inform. I wouldn't even touch the pictures, much less look at them. I'd say, "Why are you showing me these pictures?" They'd say, "Maybe we can help you out." I said, "Yeah, like helping me get killed."

After being in Milan a few months, I became friendly with the woman in charge of the food service. She told me to meet her in the kitchen and when I got there, she said, "Come walk with me Jack and you'll bring back some cookies for the fellas." She gave me a 10-pound box of cookies which I carried back to the shed where I worked. She also gave me some other things, none of which were anybody else's business. I took out a few cookies for the guard and the three guys I worked with, and I brought the rest of the cookies out into the open space where everybody was sitting. I said, "Help yourself," and went back into my shed.

A half hour later, one of the guys I worked with came in and asked me, "What did you do?" I told him I didn't know what he was talking about. "Some guys out there are mad at you," he said, and I said, "Mad at what?" He said it was something about the cookies, so I went out there and six black guys were looking at me. A guard was sitting at his desk, about 30 feet away from me, and I asked him "What's going on?" He pointed to two guys and said, "They think you took their cookies." I asked him if he was serious and he said yeah. I walked up to the two guys and said, "What!" One of them said, "You took some of my cookies when you brought the box into your shed first, man." I told him that whatever I did in my shed was none of his business, and then I went off on him.

"You, who I presume to be an adult man, had the audacity, even though you probably don't know the meaning of that word, to tell the guard that I took cookies? You're a fucking imbecile!" When he started raising his voice, it drew other inmates out of their sheds, along with a couple of other guards. This is what passes for entertainment to a lot of guys in prison, but I had good reason to be doing what I did. When I found out this guy was in there for killing his wife, it created the kind of moment that I used to live for. I said, "You're a real man among men, you fucking moron. You not only kill a woman, but you're a stool pigeon, too. You must be real proud of yourself, you motherfucker."

I harassed this poor excuse for a man for the next four days. I did it in the meal line because guards didn't pay attention to guys who were standing in line. He'd be surrounded by other guys and I'd never stand more than three or four feet away from him when I spoke. "How does it feel to kill a woman, tough guy? Don't you want to brag about it, you motherfucker." Then I'd look at other guys and say, "Hey you know this tough guy here, he killed his wife and then he accused me of taking his cookies." He said, "Come on man leave me alone." "Leave you alone," I said, "You're a piece of shit, and if everybody doesn't know it already, they soon will." After that, he never said a word to me.

On the second day of my harassment campaign, I was approached by a gang member who told me my reason for doing this was valid. "Go ahead and do it," he said, "because nobody is going to mess with you on behalf of this guy." They didn't like that he had killed a woman, and I thanked him for telling me. Lo and behold, on the fifth day, the putz finally checked himself into segregation, which is another word for the Hole. That's what cowards do when their first and strongest impulse is to kill a guy who doesn't back down from them. He chose the Hole over taking me on and even his friends didn't respect that. As for me, I couldn't let these guys think I stole anything. It's the kind of thing you have to deal with in prison, and the sooner I nipped that in the bud, the better.

A similar thing happened when an Italian guy showed up and made out like he was important. I noticed he didn't hang around many white people and I wondered why. Anyway, months later someone told him about my amusement park concept and he said he'd like to talk to me about it. He told me his brother was a casino boss in Las Vegas. "Oh, what a great idea," he said. "My brother's got the connections and he can put that right on the Strip." I said "cool," but his comment told me he was a bullshit artist and I've always hated bullshitters. As time went on, he said some other things which showed me he was even more of a bullshitter than I originally thought. I was looking for an opportunity to test him and I got it.

A black inmate told me this guy wanted to borrow some money from him to spend at the commissary, and that he would pay him back next month. He asked me what I thought about loaning the guy money and I told him, "Do what you want, but I'm pretty sure you'll never get your money back." I said that because I knew it would get back to him. Sure enough, that night we were out in the yard and I saw him walking toward me. I got up and told him to follow me to the other side of the handball court where no one could see us. He said, "Did you tell that guy I couldn't be trusted?" I think he was expecting me to deny it, but I said, "You're damn right I did, you blowhard motherfucker you. You say you're gonna put a 2.5 mile track on 800 acres of the most valuable property in the world? What are you, a moron? Do you think you're talking to an imbecile? Go fuck yourself." He checked himself into the Hole that night and I never saw him again.

I caught a break by serving my final 18 months at the co-ed prison in Lexington, Kentucky. Everyone in the federal system wanted to go there or to Ft. Worth, Texas, the only two co-ed prisons in the country. It was a minimum-security place where the cells lacked metal bars and inmates were allowed to wear street clothes. Men and women were housed in different buildings but they could mingle in the prison yard, and at breakfast, lunch, and dinner. Inmates could hold hands but they weren't supposed to do anything else. I don't know who came up with the idea for co-ed prisons, but I'm extremely grateful to whoever it was.

If you're a guy, imagine doing your prison time alongside women. Everything you might possibly think of doing in a situation like that happened at Lexington. Inmates would look around to see who they might hook up with. Everyone knew who belonged to whom, just like on the street. At night, couples would take a walk around the yard and find a place where they could fool around while someone looked out for guards. Most people were discreet and the warden turned a blind eye to it because it was calm and laid back at Lexington. There were some fights, but the vast majority of inmates were careful not to give anyone a reason to send them back to their previous prison.

A lot of guards used the threat of sending you back as leverage to control you. One day a guard saw a pair of pants on the floor near my bunk and said something about sending me back to Milan. "Then send me back," I said, knowing he'd never write me up for something as trivial as that. Another time, I got what they call a shot, which is a disciplinary action. They found a lightbulb in my locker during a routine search of my area and the guard asked me if I bought it or if it was issued to me. When I said it was neither, he told me it was contraband. I said, "Look, it was available and you and everybody in this unit knows that I read a lot." He said, "I'll tell you what, I'll let it go if you sweep up the day room." I told him to write up the shot. I embarrassed him by not backing down, so he felt he had to write it up to protect his sterling reputation.

Sure enough, I got called into the Lieutenant's Office where you get an opportunity to present your side of the story. "What do you have to say for yourself," he said. "I've been down for almost four years now," I said, "and this is one of the pettiest things I've ever seen. Everybody knows I read a lot." The lieutenant looked at me and said, "Do me a favor and get the hell out of here."

I was in a 9-man cell when I noticed a little skinny kid sitting on a bottom bunk. He was about 5'2", weighed maybe 90 pounds, and didn't speak English. I asked one of my cellmates where he came from, and learned his name was Georgie and he had been on the Mariel Boatlift. The movie, *Scarface*, depicted the boatlift perfectly. Fidel Castro emptied out his prisons and mental institutions and crowded them onto boats which were bound for Miami. But because President Reagan had closed the federal mental institutions, he transferred almost every boatlift survivor to federal prison.

Most guys kept their distance from Georgie, a guy who had nothing but the clothes on his back and a comb, a toothbrush, a small tube of toothpaste and some soap that the prison had given him. The next time I went to the commissary, I bought some essentials and some snacks and placed them on his bunk. I suggested to a couple of other guys that they do the same, and he apparently learned that I was behind it.

I had gotten into an argument with a big, well-built guy from Argentina. It wasn't that big of a deal but everyone saw it. The next thing I knew, I was walking upstairs from the day room when I saw a bunch of guys in the hallway. I opened the door and one guy said, "You better get in there." Georgie was swinging an iron and I saw he was aiming at the Argentinian with whom I had argued. One inmate said, "He's sticking up for you." I said, "Sticking up for what?" As soon as I said it, I understood what Georgie was doing, or at least why he was doing it. I said, "Georgie, stop!" I picked him up and carried him back to our cell and put him on his bunk. I waved my finger from side to side, and said, "Thank you, but you can't do that."

A couple of minutes later, I found out what had taken place before I got there. The Argentinian was ironing a shirt when Georgie picked up the iron and put it right on the guy's bare chest, all because he had the nerve to argue with me. Even to a guy as big as this Argentinian was, a 90-pound crazy man is just as dangerous, if not more so, than anybody else. I told the guy to leave it alone and he did, and in the end, nobody ratted Georgie out.

No inmate was ever allowed to touch an in-house phone in any prison and you'd be in big trouble if you did. Guards would have to double up when they did their nightly count, and every cellhouse would be left without a guard for about 10 minutes. During one of those counts, a guy came running down the stairs looking for the guard. He said a guy was having an epileptic fit and it was bad. I picked up the in-house phone and I said, "I'm an inmate, there's no guard in here and a guy is having an epileptic fit on the second floor." As I said that, I heard a click and the lieutenant got on the line. He said, "Gail, is that you?", and I responded by saying yes. At that point, he shouted "Go." A few seconds later, several guards and medical personnel came rushing in and did their job.

A couple of days later, I was walking past the case manager's office, a guy who despised me, and I took that opportunity to knock on his door. I said, "I might have helped save a guy's life. I'd like you to put that in my jacket so there'll be at least one positive thing in it." I knew he would say no and he did, but I just wanted to bust his balls.

14

SAVING GAIL TILE

SHORTLY BEFORE MY parole date, my father told me that he had stage four lung cancer. I was afraid I wouldn't be paroled before he passed, so I petitioned the prison system for a three-day furlough.

The parole structure back then was different than it is now. They paroled you after serving one third of your sentence, making it a matter of simple arithmetic. Adjusting for leap years, I had been sentenced to 5,114 days in prison, meaning I would qualify for parole after serving 1,702 days, which amounted to four years and eight months. As it turned out, my parole and furlough were scheduled within days of each other. My release date was set for December 28, 1983, and the furlough was for December 23-26. Correct me if I'm wrong, but wouldn't you think someone in the prison system might have questioned the necessity of having me return to prison for nights 1701 and 1702, especially given the circumstances? It wasn't like they had a going-away party planned for me and had already paid for the room.

Bureaucrats are like robots, no matter where they work. They could have moved my release date up a couple of days, and nobody would have cared if they had. I had never caused any trouble and I kept the peace on so many occasions that if anyone was going to be the recipient of a little goodwill, it should have been me. I'm pretty sure it never crossed any of their minds because they punish inmates every day they're behind bars.

You have to call your parole officer as soon as you get out. Who you get as a parole officer is something over which you have no control, but the guy they assigned to me couldn't have been nicer. He was aware that my father was terminally ill. "I met with your father and I know you have your hands full," he said. "Take care of your father and call me again in a couple of weeks." I went from spending four-and-a-half years in prison to watching my father die, with no time in between. Lenny Gail passed away two weeks after I got home. I informed my parole officer of the news and he said, "Take care of your affairs, Jack, and call me in another couple of weeks. You can meet with me at my house since we live so close, rather than going all the way downtown."

When I got to his house, we sat around the kitchen table drinking coffee and eating cookies as their two young kids ran around the house. It brought back memories of when my kids were the same age. He spent 30 minutes making sure I understood the rules. I said to him, "What happens if I'm seen shaking hands with somebody? Is that gonna get me violated?" He said, "I don't chase guys like you. I'm not gonna do something to violate you, Jack. If your parole gets violated, it's gonna be on you."

My father told me he left everything to his second wife, Beverly, because he didn't know what was going to happen to me in prison. He wanted me to benefit from his estate but he didn't want my brother to get anything. My father was refusing to see Steve and I asked him why. He said Steve told him, "I'm quitting Gail Tile to go into business for myself, and I'm going to put you out of business." I didn't want to believe my ears that a son would say that to his father, but he did, and I confronted my brother that day at a restaurant. "You actually told your father you were going to put him out of business? You actually said that to our father?" He just looked at me, and I said, "Well, you can forget about seeing him before he dies, because that's not going to happen."

Beverly never offered me a dime from my father's estate because she didn't have to. She didn't even want to give me Gail Tile & Carpet until she realized how close to bankruptcy the business was. In 1981 interest rates hit 22% and the country's building industry effectively ceased. When I took over Gail Tile, we owed the bank $250,000. They knew my whole story and to say they didn't like me was an understatement of epic proportions. I gave them a chunk of money to knock down the debt, hoping it would make them more comfortable in dealing with me.

After I got out of prison, I was just trying to exist. I was a lot more careful because everything on the street had changed. For one thing, there was nobody left anymore. Most of the guys I knew were either dead, in jail, or retired and living in warm climates. I didn't want any part of the Life and I didn't want any part of wiseguys either. I needed a break, and I got one.

I was at a floor-covering show at the Rosemont Convention Center when I saw a friend walk by. He and some other friends of mine had built the Allstate Arena and the Horizon, but I didn't know they had built this place, too. Rosemont's proximity to O'Hare Airport gave them a leg up on Chicago's McCormick Place for the convention and exhibition hall business. When my friend asked me what I was doing, I told him my father had died and I was trying to save his company. He took me into an office where another old friend was sitting. This guy loved my father and when he learned I had the company he said, "Jackie, I'm gonna help you. What nights are you open?"

Two nights later, he walked into Gail Tile with Donald Stevens, the founder and Mayor of the City of Rosemont. We had a very impressive showroom and Mr. Stevens liked what he saw. We went into my office and he asked me if I could supply 46,000 yards of carpet and have it delivered by January 3. I told him I could, not yet knowing how I was going to do that. "Alright," he said, "here's what we're gonna do. You supply the carpet and every three or four months we're gonna replace it and sell the old carpet to the public. Just give us a price."

Well, pinch me because I must be dreaming! Think about it. I didn't have to touch the carpet. I just needed to make sure that it got made and was shipped from point A to point B. All of a sudden, I was a carpet broker about to pull my dad's company out of bankruptcy. Three or four times a year I'd net $60,000 because I had a good reputation with the right people. It was the opportunity of a lifetime.

My stepmother gave me the name of a guy at Imperial Carpets. I called and told him I'd like to discuss a large order and he invited me to their showroom. He said, "Jack, I don't know. There's a town, Dalton, Georgia, where most of the carpet mills are, and the whole town closes up for two weeks around Christmas time, but for 46,000 yards of carpet, we'll open." The carpet was delivered to Rosemont on December 28th and Gail Tile was back in business. I would have doubled or tripled the business in no time because Rosemont kept right on growing. There would have been many more tile and carpet contracts coming my way and the Convention Center job was just the beginning.

When I brought the Rosemont contract to the bank, they put their personal feelings about me aside and gave me a $200,000 line of credit. I was feeling so good that I foolishly brought my brother back into the business. Steve and I never had any semblance of a relationship. In fact, I can't remember ever having a conversation with him even though we were less than four years apart. He was a betrayer and a deceiver his whole life, and most of my friends thought he was jealous of me. And then there was the little matter of what he said to our father. However, he was my brother and I felt sorry for him, so I overlooked what he did to my father and I rewarded his bad behavior.

Turns out my brother was lying to my bank by telling them I was skimming from the company. I had no inkling of this until I got a phone call from one of my friends in Rosemont who said he needed to talk to me face-to-face. I met him at his health club and he told me that my bank called him right before the first $100,000 check was to be cut and told him to make the check out to my bank, instead of Gail Tile. I asked him, "Why would they do that?" and he asked me the same question. Then he said, "Well, this is what they did and you better check it out."

My Rosemont friends were mad at me because they couldn't understand why the bank would do that. I tried to explain that my brother had gone to the bank and had lied about me, but the situation made them look bad in other people's eyes. Negativity like that wasn't good for their business. I couldn't really blame them for running away from me, and whatever their excuse was didn't matter. The bottom line is that situations like this ruin relationships. Nobody cares why something happens, but when it does, they go on with their lives without you.

I called the bank and they told me they were cancelling my line of credit and that I needed to find a new banking relationship. I said, "Why are you doing this to me? I'm going to do this deal three or four times a year." The banker said, "Well, that's the way we feel. Good luck to you and we'll see you later." End of story. The bankers probably thought this was a mob deal, especially when my brother used the word skimming. Once you become a felon, you rarely get the benefit of the doubt from anyone and everything works against you. They knew my background and that was strike one. For reasons I never understood, they also thought Don Stevens was mobbed up, and that was strike two. The story my brother told them was strike three.

The bankers set me up like a rank sucker and they went the extra mile to do it. They had just sold the bank but were still minding the store when they froze me out. Gail Tile owed the bank a sizeable amount of money, which I would have paid off within a year from the Rosemont contract alone. But these schmucks despised me so much that they deprived the new bank owners of many thousands of dollars just to stick it to me. I hadn't defaulted on the loan and they had no right to write off a debt that was no longer theirs. It's as if they robbed their own bank, and somehow lost the money while making their getaway. Just because they didn't get to spend the money didn't change the fact that they were bank robbers. And motherfuckers!

With my record, finding a new banking relationship was never going to happen, so that was the end of Gail Tile. I had a shot at becoming legitimate again and doing it in a big way. I coulda been a tile and carpet mogul. I coulda been somebody. My being a felon wouldn't have mattered to anyone, and it wouldn't have come up but for my little brother's vindictiveness. When Steve ruined me, he also threw away his only chance at a stable future. He sabotaged himself like that his entire life. After my father wouldn't see him, he decided he was going to get even with him, even in death, by destroying Gail Tile. With me involved, he was able to have his cake and eat it too. Oh, to have been an only child. And, by the way, the bank couldn't have been more wrong about Donald Stevens.

15
ANOTHER BETRAYAL

I WAS LIVING in Florida when my friend, Bernie Kron, offered to sell me a home in his new housing development at his cost. I had done Bernie a couple of favors that were important to him and he wanted to do something nice for me. Bernie was the father of my friend, Jeffrey, who spent a day with Rocky Marciano six months before he passed. I had also gotten Bernie some land that he needed for a housing development from a guy who didn't want to sell it to him. All I did was tell him that my friend was interested in the property and I asked him to name a price. He did, and that was that.

Being a felon made getting a mortgage almost impossible. I had been dating a woman named Sophia Sikorski for a few months and I offered to put the house in her name if she agreed to share the proceeds with me whenever it was sold. We were living in separate apartments at the time and she graciously accepted my gift of half of a new house. I figured I'd have some longevity with Sophia, but I was mistaken. We had maybe three good months together when she started staying out late and going to work early. When I asked her about it, she became increasingly belligerent with me. "I don't know what you're doing," I said to her, "but this isn't working. I don't want to be with someone who doesn't want to be with me." I told her I'd move out, we'd sell the house, split the proceeds as we had already agreed, and go our separate ways. She was fine with that.

A week after I moved out, Bernie called me to say there was a white Cadillac in my driveway during the day. He noticed it when he was making his rounds. Another week went by and Bernie told me the Cadillac was there 24 hours a day. It was obvious that Sophia wanted me out of the house so somebody else could move in. I didn't know whose car it was and I didn't care, but it hurt a lot. I got physically sick, I lost weight, and I was miserable for a couple of months. I couldn't believe that a woman would do that to me, because I'd always treated women with respect, including Sophia. Out of spite, I placed a lien on the property to prevent her from selling it, even though I didn't have a legal leg to stand on.

I had started to come out of that fog when my dear friend Ronnie Tortorella called and said he needed to see me in person. I went to his place and he told me the name of the guy living in my house was Gabriel Ponzio, someone he'd known for 20 years. I had never heard of Ponzio, but he wanted Ronnie to set up a meet with me. Ronnie said, "Sure, what do you want me to tell him?" Ponzio said, "I don't want you to tell him nothing. I want to beat him to death with a baseball bat and you're gonna set this motherfucker up for me." He actually thought Ronnie would do anything he wanted him to do. What he didn't know was that Ronnie and I had been close friends for 30 years and that I had saved his life after someone mistakenly ordered a hit on him.

I looked at Ronnie and said, "Set me up for what reason?" Ronnie shrugged and said, "He didn't say. What do you want to do?" I said, "I don't want to do anything, because this is insane. This guy must be nuts." "Regardless," said Ronnie, "what do you want to do?" Seeing the look on Ronnie's face, and knowing the meaning of his words, told me he was willing to set Ponzio up in order for me to kill him.

A week later, Ronnie invited me to dinner at his house, which he frequently did on Friday nights. I walked in and saw one of my best friends, Carlo, along with two guys that I'd never seen before. Carlo was a made guy from New York and one of the best friends

I ever had. Coppola's people looked at him for the Luca Brasi role in *The Godfather* but decided he was too good looking for the part. "Let me tell you why we're here," said Carlo. "Ronnie told me that this guy, Ponzio, wants to whack you and he wants Ronnie to set you up. What do you want to do?" I said, "Carlo, it's like I told Ronnie. I don't want to do anything." He said, "Jack, I'm a made guy, you're my friend, and I'm not gonna tolerate him disrespecting you. You don't want to do anything, I get it, we'll handle it. We don't care who he's with in Chicago. We don't need permission from anyone to deal with this prick."

Guys like Ronnie and Carlo were funny as hell but when it came to certain things in this life, nobody was more serious than they were. Carlo would have whacked Ponzio for me out of friendship, plus this was no longer just about me. Ponzio had tried to involve Ronnie in a conspiracy to commit murder and he didn't appreciate it one bit. Gabriel Ponzio never knew how close he came to getting killed over this, and the way things turned out for me, well…I think you know where I'm going with that.

As much as I appreciated my friends wanting to protect me, the whole situation seemed ridiculous. Still, I knew that Ponzio wouldn't have gone to Ronnie if he wasn't serious, so I couldn't ignore his threat. Finally, Ronnie said, "Jack, this guy's serious. What do you want to do?" I knew the look he was giving me. I said, "Ronnie, if anything were to happen to Ponzio, the Feds would be all over me for the rest of my life." My parole officer knew he was living in the house that I used to live in with my former girlfriend. And, after what happened in Memphis, every federal agent in the country thought I was a hitman.

I reminded Ronnie and Carlo that it was Sophia who did this to me, not Ponzio. She let him in because that's what she wanted. All he did was get her to kick me out of the house. Ponzio had a five-step plan: he would marry Sophia, sell my house, use the proceeds to get a bigger house which he would put in his name, divorce Sophia, and take everything of value from her. Guys like Ponzio have never worked for a living and they think everything is for free, everything is for me, me, me! Welcome to the ignorant wiseguy attitude.

One day, a Sheriff's Deputy knocked on my former front door with a subpoena for Sophia and Ponzio got into an argument with the guy. He damn near got arrested for sticking his nose in a place where it didn't belong. Ronnie's wife, Diane, told me Ponzio had dated Sophia on and off for several years before we hooked up and she always thought there was something wrong with him. She would call him an asshole to his face and he'd brag about that to other people. He was slick, rude and belligerent, but his defining characteristic was that he beat women.

Ronnie never liked Sophia. He hired her as a bartender at the club he was managing, but only because she was friends with Ronnie's wife. He had a gut feeling about her and he ended up firing her for stealing. Ronnie's motto was "steal a little, leave a lot." Sophia had the opposite philosophy. She wouldn't admit to it so he set her up by leaving her with 50 beers. When Ronnie checked the register, all 50 of the beers had been sold but only five had been rung up, so he fired her.

Years later, Diane told me that Ponzio threatened to kill Sophia every few days. He beat the hell out of her so many times that she ran away, moved back to Chicago, went into hiding, and divorced him. I had bought Sophia a doberman puppy just before I moved out and Ponzio wouldn't give her the dog. It died suddenly a few months later and Sophia was sure he had killed it. To be honest, I felt worse for the dog than I did about her.

Betrayal had become a cruelly recurrent theme by this point in my life, and I wrote the whole situation off. I returned to Chicago in June, 1991, when my father's second wife and one of her daughters were both diagnosed with cancer. My decision to move 1,300 miles away from Florida had nothing to do with my ex-girlfriend or my ex-house. I figured Ponzio would stop wanting to kill me once he realized just one of the following three things: 1) I had moved 1,300 miles away; 2) My lien was invalid because I had no legally binding interest in the house; and 3) It was sheer lunacy to even consider killing anyone over something like this.

16
WHAT ARE THE ODDS?

ATF SPECIAL AGENT James Delorto was looking for drug trafficking leads when his Confidential Informant (CI), Joe Granata, got a call from his cousin, Gabriel Ponzio. Granata had been involved in the mob since the 1960's, and began informing on wiseguys in the early 1980's to avoid going to prison. The Feds paid him $35 a day for his part in a number of investigations, plus bonuses for setting up large purchases of drugs and weapons with organized crime figures, while wearing a wire. Granata participated in 22 federal investigations and was paid $64,345 by the IRS, DEA and FBI over just one two-year period. He got paid for arrests rather than convictions, and became an ATF snitch in March, 1990.

The conversation between Granata and Ponzio took place about two weeks after I returned to Chicago. Ten minutes into that call, Ponzio told Granata that his girlfriend's former lover had placed a lien on her house, and he wanted his cousin to make the lien disappear. "His name's Jackie Gail and he says we owe him $18,000. I figure he has about five thousand coming, and I was gonna give it to him, Joey. If I was making money I don't give a fuck. This dumb motherfucker. I want to fuck him real good. You have to come here and grab his son, but I'm afraid that if I grab his kid he'll beef."

During that call, Ponzio and Granata talked about several illegal activities, but none were anywhere near as serious as kidnapping a child. Agent Delorto overheard that threat and he ignored it. Excuse me? Don't you think a federal agent would have immediately informed his co-workers, his superiors, and me, that my son might be in danger so that I could protect him? Wouldn't a federal crimefighter arrest or at least question the guy who made the threat? Delorto and his fellow ATF agents didn't do either of those things because they didn't care. Like everybody else, they had an agenda, and their agenda was to punish me for refusing to become a government informant back in 1978.

Everything the ATF did to me was illegal from the very beginning. The moment James Delorto heard my name, the ATF attached themselves to a murder conspiracy hatched by Gabriel Ponzio and made it their own, with one important change. They sent a known hitman to entrap me, rather than to murder me. They told Granata that his job was to involve me in a crime by any means necessary.

Agents refuse to accept that some guys won't inform on others in order to stay out of prison, and I refused to do that 13 years earlier. That's why Delorto took another run at me when he heard my name. He wanted to punish me for not flipping after my first arrest, as if serving four years and eight months in a federal prison wasn't punishment enough. It's as simple as that. I wasn't being targeted for anything I did. I was targeted for not being a rat. That's when Joe Granata went from being a government informant to an ATF pawn, and the distinction is important. A CI is a law enforcement asset who wears a wire to provide evidence against individuals who are the subject of ongoing criminal investigations. A pawn, on the other hand, is used by his puppet masters to create the appearance of criminal activity for an agent's own personal agenda.

At this point, Delorto paid a visit to the U.S. Attorneys whose names are on the cover of this book, and asked them if they were interested in taking another run at Jackie Gail. Gary Shapiro and Mitchell Mars said, "Just tell us what you need." They gave Delorto permission to use his CI to create whatever scenario he needed in order to entrap me. The "thin blue line" is law enforcement's version of omerta. To put it another way, what takes place in a U.S. Attorney's office, stays in that U.S. Attorney's office.

Delorto's next step was to find another CI who knew me well enough to make an introduction for Granata. Out of the blue, I got a call from an old friend, Richie Urso, who I hadn't seen in 15 years, and I wondered how he got my number. Richie knew everybody and everybody liked him. He was in the trucking business and as far as I knew, he was never a wiseguy. We met at Myron and Phil's in Lincolnwood where I asked him, "What's going on?" He said, "Jack, I don't really know. I was just asked to hook you up with a guy named Joe Granata who wants to talk to you about a house in Florida." Right away, I knew the only person on the planet who could have arranged this was Gabriel Ponzio.

Richie gave me Granata's phone number and we spent the rest of the time reminiscing over a cocktail. I had no idea why Richie would be contacting me over this, but I didn't know what he had been doing for the previous 15 years, either. When we got up to leave, I tried to give Richie a hug and he stiffened up as if he were wearing a wire. Flags don't get any redder than that, and it gave me pause.

I called Granata a couple of days later. He told me he was representing his cousin, Gabriel Ponzio, and said he wanted to discuss my house in Florida. I arranged to meet him at the Blue Angel restaurant on Milwaukee Avenue in Chicago and told him to look for a good looking guy with gray hair. I got there a few minutes early and went to take a leak. I was on guard because I didn't know if he was going to be alone or if he was going to bring help. The only thing I was certain of was that his cousin wanted to kill me and Granata was the guy he sent to do it.

Granata introduced himself and sat down at my booth. I asked him what this was about, and he said, "You're gonna come off the lien that you placed on my cousin's house, Jack." That's the way he said it, like he was giving me an order. I looked at him and smiled, and repositioned my feet so I'd be ready to crack him if necessary. I said, "And who's gonna make me do that Joe, you? Cause if that's the case, do it now!" I figured he'd back down and he did. Granata was an easy guy to read. Hitman or not, he looked weak to me. I used to eat guys like Joe Granata and looking back on that first meeting, I probably should have knocked his head off.

Having been disabused of the notion that I was some kind of wuss, Granata pivoted to a different tact. He said he was doing this as a favor to his cousin who was really an asshole. I wasn't buying his bullshit, but I let him talk. He mentioned Richie Urso's name like the three of us were childhood friends. When he finally shut up, I told him exactly what happened with the house and said, "Joe, if you want to put yourself in this position, that's up to you." And then I left. Granata called me the next day and I told him I wasn't going to withdraw the lien. I didn't think I'd hear from him again, but since Ponzio wanted me dead, I knew I couldn't be sure of that.

When Granata spoke with Ponzio the following day, he was working off of the ATF's script. "Find out where he's at," he told his cousin, "and then you call cousin Joey. I'm gonna set him up, I'm gonna take care of this guy and when I do, you'll owe me a favor." Granata wasn't talking about killing me, but Ponzio didn't know that. He also didn't know his cousin was a longtime CI for the federal government or that his threat to kidnap my son was on tape. He needn't have worried, though, because James Delorto was more inclined to thank Ponzio for mentioning my name than he was to punish him for threatening to kidnap my son or threatening to kill me which he also said during that conversation, though you had to understand mobspeak to recognize it.

The last thing I would ever do is back away from a threat like Ponzio's under any circumstances, and that was my approach during this entire episode. If somebody threatened to kill you, you could deal with it in one of three ways. You could ignore the threat, you could call the police, or you could handle it on your own. You'd have to be an idiot to ignore the threat and going up against a hitman by yourself is something few people in their right mind would ever consider doing. I'm betting you'd call the police like any normal person would. Well, I guess I'm not normal because I would never do that. I was friends with hundreds of cops but I never needed any of them, or anyone else, to look out for me. If I had gone to the police with Ponzio's threat, the people I knew would have looked at me like I was a rat, a term which I do not like and rarely use. However, I guarantee you that's how it would have been perceived, which is one of the reasons why I never even considered going to the police.

I had been away from Chicago for 12 years when I contacted what was left of the Outfit. Most of the guys I knew were gone by this time. The guys that were still around didn't really know me, but they knew of me, and that's why they agreed to give me an audience. After making some inquiries, they told me to meet them on a certain day at the kind of unassuming looking Italian-American social club where wiseguys used to hang out. The boss and an associate of his were waiting for me at a table in the back of the room. I told the boss I was being threatened by a guy with connections and I asked him if there was a hit out on me. He said, "That's ridiculous, Jack. There's nobody who's gonna put a hit out on you."

I told him that a guy named Gabriel Ponzio had threatened me, and the guy he sent to kill me was Joe Granata. "Stay away from this guy, Granata," he said. "He's a nutcase and he will kill you. He likes killing people. You got a problem with that guy, do what you got to do. You don't have to worry about nothing because nobody here's gonna care." He didn't say I should whack Granata in so many words, but he was telling me it wouldn't be a problem if I did. Then he told me Ponzio was connected to Paul Ricca, and that was more significant than what he told me about Granata. Not many people know about Paul Ricca anymore but after Al Capone went away for tax evasion, Ricca and Tony Accardo took over the Chicago Outfit. I thanked the boss and he wished me well.

I felt better after that meeting than I did before it. I left there secure in the knowledge that the Outfits in New York and Chicago were on my side and of like minds. All I had to do was give the word and Ponzio and Granata would have slept with the gefilte fish. I decided to stay away from Granata thinking that the situation with his cousin would work itself out once cooler heads prevailed. Still, I couldn't forget that Ponzio wanted me dead over something that only a crazy person would think was a capital crime. The problem is, you never know what a crazy person is going to do.

17

PURE FICTION

I DIDN'T HEAR from Granata again until he called me in September, wanting to be my friend. "I heard good things about you, Jack. You're a hell of a guy," he said. "I need to be around somebody like you. How about we meet up again?" I figured this meant Gabriel Ponzio still wanted to kill me. I never cowered from anybody and I was still waiting for Joe to make a move. Hitmen will tell you anything to get you to a location where they can do their jobs as quietly as possible, so I made it a point to always meet Granata in public places. I was also pretty sure he didn't have the balls to come after me alone.

On October 10, we met at the Mirage Restaurant in Rosemont, and Granata was sitting in a booth when I got there. Joe Granata was the most ignorant sounding person I had ever heard. There was only so much of him that I could take at one sitting, which is why our meetings never lasted more than 20 or 25 minutes. At one point, he offered me a kilo of cocaine if I'd release the lien on my house. The first time I met with him he tried to muscle me off the lien, but now he was offering me drugs with a street value of at least $20,000. A couple of minutes later, he told me he finally realized what a prick his cousin was. He said Gabe deserved to be killed, as did Sophia, because of what she did to me. Who tells a total stranger he'd like to kill his own family members, or kill anyone for that matter? A crazy person or a government snitch, that's who.

Granata was either trying to lull me into complacency, or someone was pulling his strings. This situation could have only been one of two things. I was either being targeted for death by a couple of stupid wiseguys or I was being set up by the federal government for no legitimate reason. If that's what the Feds were trying to do, I was confident I could embarrass them in a court of law no matter what their motivations were. All I had done was waste a little of my time with an ignoramus who said he wanted to be my partner in crime and that, in and of itself, is not a crime. I was only talking to this half wit because I had good reason to believe he was sent by Gabriel Ponzio to kill me, which, in fact, he was. Other than that, I figured I had nothing to worry about, and that included the Feds.

Our October 10 meeting would be hugely important, not because of anything I said, but because of what the Feds did after the meeting. Granata kept suggesting crimes we could commit together, in addition to killing Ponzio, and I just let him talk. ATF special agents Matthew Gorecki and James Delorto were waiting for me to incriminate myself but I think they knew that wasn't going to happen. In true ATF fashion, they justified their pursuit of me by making something up. Agent Gorecki told his superiors that the audio tape machine had failed to record a single word of our conversation. Then he submitted a written statement by Joe Granata and an almost identical letter of his own attesting to the story that Granata supposedly told him immediately after meeting with me. This was Granata's statement:

"I am 51 and have known Jack Gail for approximately eight months and I know him to be a convicted felon in possession of firearms and in the business of selling cocaine. On October 10, 1991, I told Special Agent Matthew L. Gorecki that Jack Gail called me at my house and told me that he wanted to meet with me in person regarding something important. Gail told me that he did not want to talk about it on the telephone. We agreed to meet in the parking lot at the Howard Johnson motel in Schiller Park, Illinois.

"Gail asked me if I could give to him one kilogram of cocaine on credit. He explained he wanted to help an old friend out who was hurting financially. Gail said that he would be able to sell the cocaine quickly by using his restaurant in Pompano, Florida. I first told him that he was crazy for asking me to give it to him on credit. Gail then said that he was desperate and that he would appreciate it if I could help him out. Gail said that he would be responsible if something went wrong.

"At this, Gail told me that he was planning to go to Florida in order to kill Gabriel Ponzio over a dispute in which Ponzio stole Gail's girlfriend while he (Gail) was in Chicago. When Gail told me that he was planning to go to Florida on November 3, 1991, to do the job on Ponzio, I told him that I would go with him to help. Gail told me that he had all his own guns to take care of the job. On this note, we ended our conversation and agreed that we would keep in touch. Before Gail got out of my car, he told me that he would be waiting for my answer on the cocaine."

Granata's entire statement was false. First of all, he knew me for three months, not eight. Second, I never initiated any contact with Granata, because he always called me. If I ever contacted him, it was only to return his call. I never wanted anything from him and I never took anything from him. Third, I wasn't in possession of firearms. Fourth, I was never in the business of selling cocaine. Fifth, I never asked him for a kilo of cocaine. Sixth, I had already sold my hot dog stand and I never sold drugs in my life. Seventh, at no point did I ever tell him I wanted to kill or otherwise harm Gabriel Ponzio. Joe brought up the subject four of the five times I met with him, but I never did. And on a personal note, I've never been desperate in my life.

Furthermore, it was obvious to me that Joe Granata didn't write his statement because he never spoke in complete or coherent sentences. Contrast his so-called recollections of that October 10 meeting with these excerpts from the transcript of one of his conversations with me, and you'll see just how inarticulate a human being can be.

- *"My brother had a head roll goin'. What was it? The other night. The day before, and he was makin' my head like, got a haircut. He says, don't fuck with.....Ha ha."*

- *"A kee. Two point two kees to a pound. A lot of money there."*

- *"You'll see what Big Don. Look at me and grab me. I used to have him with one of my hookers. "That one Joe." He'll grab me, "What the fuck you doin? What the fuck Don? What do you wanna do Don"? I stay away. They're heated. I don't want nothin'. I tell him, "I don't want ya to even fuckin' look at me, man." I tell 'em right to their face."*

- *"Oh. Well anyways, I used to go to them, ate at the gas station when Joe was there and all these guys were there. I said, how can that motherfucker, and he's, he'd be outside fillin' his car up. He always walk and you guys had to...?" Joe would, "Eeeeh, why you wanna? Why you causing trouble? And Joe's, Eeeeh. Fuck you. I walk away."*

Painful, absolutely painful. I would have known Granata didn't write his statement if I had seen it at the time of my trial. I don't know if my attorney saw it either because he refused to let me be involved in my own defense. Those two unverifiable and demonstrably untrue, sworn statements from Granata and Gorecki would be used to establish probable cause and to build their entire case against me. A competent attorney would have destroyed the State's case and the credibility of Granata and Gorecki by proving that nothing they said about me in those statements was true.

I was about to request a second meeting with the Outfit when their people called and invited me to lunch at a restaurant on Lawrence Avenue, near Kimball. They knew a lot more about me now than they did at the time of our first meeting, and the boss was impressed. "We heard good things about you, Jack, the way you stood up, you did a lot of time, you didn't hurt anybody, you got a good reputation." He told me they weren't absolutely certain, but there was talk that Granata was a rat. "You do what you got to do, Jack." It was clear they wanted Granata whacked and they were giving me the okay to do it.

Prior to Gabriel Ponzio sending Joe Granata after me, I was developing an indoor flea market which would sell motorized vehicles of all kinds. At the time, the economy was bad and the auto industry was on its ass. I found a 150,000 square foot building in the northwest suburb of Itasca that had been built on spec but had yet to find a renter. The Georgia-based builders of the property liked my plan and were willing to work with me on the rent and the renovations.

I wanted to do what had never been done. There were auctions for auto dealers which weren't open to the public, and there were sites similar to what I had in mind, but they had limited inventory, and usually sold only cars and pickups. The operators took a piece of the action from both the buyer and the seller. At my place, I would only get a piece from the seller. More importantly, the building was big enough to accommodate people's cars, trucks, SUVs, motorcycles, RVs, boats and truck cabs where the general public could buy and sell vehicles in a comfortable atmosphere. Owners would put a price on their vehicle, along with information about it and how to make an appointment for a test drive. There would be vendors selling food, automotive related items, and who knows what else. It would be warm in winter and cool in the summer and I knew we'd get a lot of traffic once it was up and running. People love their vehicles and they always have.

The project hinged on getting investors to back me, and there's the rub. Building a successful business is tough enough under any circumstances, but it's far more difficult if you're a felon. No bank is going to loan you money because the entire establishment looks down on felons. You need to raise the money on your own and that is a huge challenge. People were interested in investing but they all seemed a little reticent. I remember a friend of mine asking me, "Who's gonna give you money for that?" I said, "What do you mean." He said, "Jack, who's gonna loan you money?" I said, "Say what you mean, please." Finally, he said, "What if you don't pay them back? What are they gonna do about it?" He had a good point and I'll tell you why.

As soon you get indicted, you're done, you're finished. People back away from you and you'll never see them again, at least not in this lifetime. They're skeptical of anything and everything you say or do, as if they've been laboring under a false impression from the moment they met you. You're automatically a liar and you can't be trusted. Believe me, I've witnessed it for the past 40 years and I'm convinced it's as much a part of the human condition as betrayal is.

I mentioned my idea to Granata at our next meeting on December 2. I only brought it up so I could get him to shut up for a couple of minutes. He said he'd like to see the site, but a few minutes later he started talking about killing his cousin again. Without responding to him directly, I sarcastically said, "Can you get me an Uzi?" and he said he could. Agent Gorecki thought he might finally have me. The very next day, he sent a *Request For Use Of Props* to the ATF's Chicago district office. The document was reviewed and signed by Gorecki's Group Supervisor, John J. Ruggero and approved and signed by the Special Agent in Charge, Joseph J. Vince Jr. This was no rogue operation, it was simply the way the ATF went about their business.

Jack Gail is a known convicted felon and organized crime figure who is in the business of selling cocaine and believed to be in possession of firearms. It is also believed by the Highland Park PD that Jack Gail is a prime suspect in the murder of former Chicago police officer, Sam Canzoneri.

Information has been received from CI 33116-20 that Gail is regularly in possession of firearms and deals in the sale of large quantities of cocaine which he obtains from an unknown Colombian individual. Gail has, on various occasions, made offers to sell cocaine to CI 33116-20 while making it obvious that he had a handgun on his person.

It has become known to ATF that Jack Gail is a longtime organized crime associate and has been suspected by other local law enforcement agencies to be involved in various "Outfit" related contract murders.

Assistant U.S. Attorneys Gary Shapiro and Mitchell Mars of the Strike Force Division have expressed a strong interest in prosecuting Gail on Federal firearms and narcotics violations pursuant to an ATF investigation. Furthermore, Assistant State's Attorney George Strickland of Lake County is interested in connecting Gail to the Sam Canzoneri murder.

CI 33116-20 has kept in close contact with Gail. On 12/2/91, Gail told CI that he wanted to purchase an Uzi submachine gun in order to murder an individual known as Gabriel Ponzio who lives in Pompano Beach, Florida. Gail related that he was going to be in Florida from 12/19 to 12/30 and that he was planning on killing Ponzio during that time frame. CI told Gail that he thought he would be able to obtain a fully automatic Uzi for him to purchase.

This will be a reverse buy/bust in which the defendant, Jack Gail, has solicited CI to purchase a Title II weapon, namely, an Uzi submachine gun. By purchasing this weapon, Gail will be in violation of Title 26. Furthermore, since Gail is a convicted felon, he will also be in violation of Title 8. This prop is needed in order to prove these violations.

Gail will be arrested as he is attempting to purchase the firearm. Surveillance will be conducted by ATF special agents, and enough personnel will be involved to ensure that more than adequate cover will be provided. This will prevent any possible rip-off by the subject and maintain security of the prop. The prop will be returned upon completion of the undercover contract.

Slander is too mild a word to describe Gorecki's claims against me. If I were to redact all of the lies in that memo with a thick black marker, the only thing left would be my name. Everything he wrote about me was pure fiction, authored by a man with a profound sense of malice. Much of Gorecki's request was pulled from his fictionalized account of my October 10 meeting with Granata. Gorecki also made up several new things and they weren't minor. The part about me being a major cocaine seller, and always carrying a gun when I conducted business were either figments of his imagination or pulled from somebody else's file. The worst of his lies was that I was a prime suspect in the murder of Sam Canzoneri and various other unspecified contract murders.

No one questioned any part of his statement and Gorecki got his request approved. The ATF's malevolence toward me was staggering, and all because I wouldn't inform on anybody. If the ATF wasn't breaking any laws by doing this to me, then we definitely need some new laws. I never conspired to destroy anybody, but agents Delorto and Gorecki did, and who knows how many other people they did it to.

Apart from the many fabrications in Gorecki's statement, one thing stood out to me. He mentioned that Assistant U.S. Attorneys Gary Shapiro and Mitchell Mars had a "strong interest in prosecuting me on Federal firearms and narcotics violations pursuant to an ATF investigation." Shapiro and Mars weren't investigating me for anything, but they, too, wanted to put me in prison by any means necessary. Shapiro was the guy who declared in open court that I had been involved in the assassination of Sam Giancana. Mars was the guy who had me held in contempt when I refused to testify before a grand jury after my first conviction. Shapiro and Mars wanted to destroy me because of my unwillingness to inform on Dominic Santarelli, a guy who at this point was in federal prison. As far as they were concerned, there was no statute of limitations for the crime of not cooperating with the Feds.

18
SAY HELLO TO MY LITTLE UZI

DELORTO COULDN'T WIRETAP me because the ATF had no probable cause to do so. Wiretaps are considered so sensitive that federal law bars the government from even seeking court approval for one unless a top prosecutor has personally authorized the request. The law exists to make sure that wiretap authority is only used when totally appropriate. Delorto was able to sidestep the wiretap process because the only guy he was interested in having me talk to was Joe Granata, and Granata was already wired.

Delorto formally requested the use of a tape recorder, a transmitter with remote receiver, and a telephone induction coil for his CI. His application didn't mention the fact that he had recorded every one of my prior conversations with Granata, without seeking permission, which is why he felt the need to cover his ass. The reasons the ATF cited for their surveillance of me were 1) "to provide protection for their undercover informant," 2) "to preclude the defense of entrapment," and 3) "to gather evidence of the primary violation of a felon in possession of a firearm."

The fact that I had a criminal record basically took away my ability to claim entrapment. In order to use entrapment as a defense, you have to have no predisposition to commit a crime. I didn't have any such predisposition, but my prior conviction could have been used to argue otherwise. What made it worse was the fact that there is no legal use for silencers, the crime for which I first got busted. In Delorto's mind, that made me fair game and made it easier for him to justify coming after me, even though I had paid my debt to society.

The ATF tried to get me to participate in a criminal conspiracy with Granata. In legal terms, a conspiracy is an agreement between two or more people to commit a crime. Conspiracies are easy to prove because the crime is committed merely by planning it and doing an overt act in furtherance of it. Let's say someone suggests that you and he rob the currency exchange on the corner of such and such in downtown Chicago. It's not your idea and it's not something you'd ever consider doing. Later on, the guy comes back to you and says, "Look, I just want to drive past the place and see if they have more than one entrance." If you drive around the Currency Exchange, you've engaged in a criminal conspiracy to commit robbery. That's the way the law works and ignorance is no defense.

Granata and I met again a couple of weeks later because he wanted to see my vehicle flea market site. I thought the other shoe might drop that day and I was prepared to give him a beating. We met at a restaurant in Rosemont and drove to Itasca in his car. On the way there, he reached into the back seat and lifted a blanket that was covering an Uzi. Somebody obviously thought my request to Granata was a serious one. I didn't say anything and Granata suggested we drive down to Florida to kill Ponzio. He offered to provide me with the guns of my choice and I didn't respond to that either.

I had taken a laxative the night before and it hit me on the way out there. I asked Granata to stop at a gas station so I could use the restroom, and when I came out, I saw that he had turned his car around. He started driving back to Rosemont and I said, "What about the building?" He said, "That's okay, you can show me another time." I think he got scared and his survival instinct kicked in. A part of me wanted him to make a move that day and every time I think about not cracking him, it frustrates me. The thing is, when you're on parole, you don't want to be an aggressor. That's a problem for a guy like me because I would have always punched someone in the face if I had to defend myself, in spite of the possible consequences.

When we got back to Rosemont, we walked to the rear of the car. I bent Granata over the trunk, not heavy, but heavy enough to show him I was serious. I put my finger on his throat and said, "I don't want that Uzi, Joe. I don't need that and I don't want anything from you!" I treated him like the rat I'd been told he was. My not taking the bait must have infuriated Delorto and Gorecki because the ATF had meticulously planned this encounter. There were probably 20-25 cops and agents in that parking lot, even though the Uzi was unloaded and I was unarmed. The only thing that mattered to them was my taking possession of the gun, thus committing the crimes of illegal possession of a Class 2 weapon and violating the terms of my parole.

It had been five months since my first meeting with the ATF's pawn and they had nothing but my sarcasm to show for it. I'd like to know how many man hours were invested in this little vendetta of theirs, but I doubt that they kept count. Logically, you would think it was time for Delorto to cut his losses, but he took on partners instead. Mitchell Mars told Delorto and Gorecki that Lake County Assistant State's Attorney George Strickland was obsessed with solving the 1989 murder of Sam Canzoneri. That gave Delorto and Gorecki a local prosecutor who wanted to bust me as much as they did. When Delorto told Strickland that the ATF was investigating me for that crime, Lake County effectively said, "Where do we sign up?" Strickland had already made up his mind that I was the killer and I've been told he went to his grave thinking that.

If there was any possible way that George Strickland could have charged me with Sam's murder, he would have done it. I later learned Lake County never looked at anyone other than me and his wife for that crime. They wanted that high-profile case solved and that was their agenda when they joined forces with the ATF. To a prosecutor like George Strickland, closing murder cases is the holy grail of career advancement. By partnering with Lake County, Delorto was able to withhold key information about Joe Granata, while providing Strickland and his associates with plausible deniability.

Several months ago I had a chance meeting with one of Highland Park's detectives at the time of my arrest. I was with a good friend of mine, and this detective didn't know who I was. He started telling my friend about the Canzoneri murder investigation. "We had the killer," he said, "but the guy wouldn't crack." He was talking about me! I mean, what are the odds of that happening?

I thought about it for a couple of days and asked my friend to arrange a meeting with the guy. When we met, he was surprised and a little embarrassed. I was a gentleman, as always, and told him I just wanted to have a conversation. "You don't appear to be angry," he said. "People are going to be surprised you're not angry." He said the ATF told Lake County that I was "more than capable" of killing Canzoneri. He asked me if I had killed Sam because he still believed I did, based entirely on what George Strickland told the Highland Park police department. Quite a few Lake County officials were convinced that Sam's wife had whacked him, and that I was in on it. "You were jockeying her," he said, which meant I was sleeping with her. "We wanted to nail you so you could flip on her. Then everybody's happy."

I asked him if that's what Strickland told him. "Yeah," he said. "They planted that shit. They set you up because they wanted to set you up." I asked him if he ever wondered why I was talking to Granata in the first place and he said no. He didn't know anything about Granata or Ponzio, he just knew I was supposed to kill a guy in Florida. That was the sum of what he knew about the whole thing. It's not the job of police officers to question their superiors. Their job is to do what they're told, and they were told I was a hitman who had killed Sam Canzoneri. All of this was a direct result of the FBI's labelling me a hitman in 1977 when their CI tried to kill me at the Memphis International Airport.

I met with Granata in mid-January after he told me he knew people who wanted in on my flea market idea. He said he wanted to make sure I understood that it was my ass on the line if their investment went south. Rather than respond, I started talking about him. I told Granata the way to make money was to be legitimate, like I was. "Joe," I said, "being involved with the shit that you're always talking about is lunacy in this day and age. There's no money in it so why take the risk?" That was the last thing Delorto and Gorecki wanted to hear. They had tried to portray me as a big-time drug dealer, and here I was lecturing their pawn on the dangers of drugs and the necessity of being legitimate.

Granata didn't care what I was saying because he wasn't there to listen. He couldn't wait until I stopped talking so he could get back to talking about crimes we should commit together. Granata said he wanted to partner with me on some big cocaine deals less than 15 seconds after I made my position on that subject as clear as I possibly could. I told him those were federal crimes he was talking about, but he kept right on trying to sell me on them. I finally said, "I'm on parole, Joe. I don't want to give any town a reason to investigate me because I don't want the government anywhere near me." He didn't respond, so I asked him why he wanted to kill his cousin. Here's how the rest of that conversation went:

Joe: Because you asked me.

Me: I never asked you. You volunteered.

Joe: I volunteered?

Me: You volunteered.

Joe: Then I won't go.

Me: I'm asking why, why you doin' this for me?

Joe: Cause I wanna be uh, your partner in business. Trust. It's up to, ya know, you don't have to have me, man.

Me: Okay.

Joe: I mean, it's, it's friendship.

Me: Okay.

Joe: Because the kid that you're goin' against, I can't stand the motherfucker. That's number one. And what he did, it's whatever you fuckin' want. Now you made me turn red.

Me: What did you ever tell him?

Joe: Who?

Me: Gabe.

Joe: Nothin'. What do you mean, what did I ever tell him?

Me: About me.

Joe: Nothin'. Nothin'. I never even, I don't think I ever brought you up with him. I don't even think I brought...

Me: He called you, right?

Joe: He asked me if I knew you. That's how it came about. He asked me if I knew a guy named Jack Gail. I said let me find out about him and that's why I reached out for Richie (Urso). I said, Rich, is this guy Jack alright? He said, Joe, that's the one you wanna be with. This kid's a money maker. I said, okay, I better play my cards right. I told my brother this kid's a good kid and I think you ought to invest in this plan of his. I'm pretty sure I'll get it, Jack. Money's the name of the game, right? So, I figured I'd make money with you.

Granata was dancing as fast as he could but I had had enough. There was never any action, so I decided it was time to end what now seemed to be a pointless exercise. Murders don't take six months to plan. He had opportunities to try to kill me but he didn't take them.

I was actually in a very good mood because I had gotten permission from my parole officer to go to Las Vegas on business at the end of January. Meanwhile, back in the van, Delorto was fuming. He had invested six months on setting me up and he still had nothing. I hadn't taken his bait, nor had I said anything incriminating, and he had to know I never would. Granata offered me drugs and I didn't bite. He thought he could get me to take possession of an Uzi, and I declined that, too. From the very start, Delorto wanted me to agree to conspire to kill Ponzio, but I never did. Kill a guy for sleeping with my girlfriend? Who thinks that way?

If I were a hitman like the FBI said I was, why the hell would I need help killing a guy? Hitmen who talk about their hits, or commit them with someone else, are asking to be either caught or whacked, so I guess Delorto thought I was either stupid, evil, or both. Enter Plan B, which was predicated on getting me to take possession of something that I thought was legal, but wasn't. The ATF set a trap, and they used $100,000 to bait it.

19

THE ARREST

JAMES DELORTO MADE sure that all anyone knew about my so-called case was what he told them. The ATF told George Strickland that Granata came to them in 1990 as a "concerned citizen" who had no criminal record and Strickland didn't question it. Delorto also lied about my interactions with Granata, and Strickland didn't question that either.

All Strickland cared about was punishing me for the Sam Canzoneri murder, one way or another. After the ATF gave him Granata's fictional summary of our October 10 meeting, he was absolutely certain that I had killed Sam. He wasn't about to doubt the Feds, especially since they told him what he wanted to hear.

The afternoon before I got arrested, April Granata called to tell me her husband had raised $100,000 and he wanted me to call him right away at a phone number she provided. When I did, Joe told me he expected to have the money by the following day, and wanted to give it to me at the Lake Forest Oasis. This could have waited until I got back from Vegas, but I decided not to wait. It was the first time we'd be meeting outside of Cook County and I thought this might be when Granata was going to make his move.

I almost took a retired detective with me. He was a good friend and it was his idea to come along. He was one of the guys the ATF wanted me to inform on the first time I went to prison. He knew about this situation and he offered to provide me with protection. "Jack," he said, "let me at least give you some cover. Not having a gun puts you at a big disadvantage, especially if more than one guy comes at you." I thought about it, but I didn't want to put him in a spot if things got violent. As it turned out, it wasn't one of my better decisions.

As I was getting ready for my meeting with Granata, law enforcement was having a meeting of their own in Vernon Hills, Illinois. It was attended by five members of the Lake County Metropolitan Enforcement Group, four ATF agents, four members of the Highland Park PD, two Lake County Assistant State's Attorneys and their pawn, Joe Granata. The DEA and the Illinois State Police had already been informed of their plan and were told what to do. Assignments were made for a "controlled reversal sale of 3.5 grams of investigative cocaine." The Feds are usually the ones buying drugs when they trap their prey but this time they were giving it away. The balls of these guys! They claimed I was a big time drug dealer, yet I had to get one night's worth of cocaine from Granata. It didn't make sense because it didn't have to make sense.

Granata, of course, was wearing a wire. The ATF supplied the Lake County agents with portable radios to monitor and record his conversation with me. At 1:10, four ATF agents and two Highland Park cops left the meeting for the 11-minute drive to the Oasis. They were told to conduct surveillance of the parking lots from their undercover vehicles. Another ATF agent made a walk-through of the Oasis. At 1:28, ATF agents Delorto and Ruggero, and prosecutors Strickland and Kornak, left the meeting for the Oasis. All four men were to remain out of sight until I was arrested, but they had no business being there in the first place. I'll bet that's the only time in their sordid careers that they did that. The fact that they needed to see me taken into custody, showed how personal this was to them.

At 1:37, Gorecki gave a Lake County agent named Middleton a black and white Reebok gym bag which contained an unloaded

.357 Ruger revolver. Middleton then unsealed the bag holding the cocaine and placed the drug in the gym bag next to the gun The items were placed on something that felt similar in size and weight to bundles of cash. They didn't want to give me any reason to open the bag because if I had, it would have ended the charade. Three minutes later, Middleton placed the gym bag under the driver's seat of Granata's undercover vehicle. Gorecki then drove to the parking lot, followed by Granata and two Lake County ATF agents in separate, unmarked vehicles.

At 1:53, Granata pulled up next to my car in the middle of the west parking lot. I had gotten there 15 minutes earlier and parked in a place where I could see everything around me. ATF agents Middleton and Kuramitsu were parked approximately 100 feet from where we were, in a direct line of sight of both of us. I noticed a car with two antennas on it and two guys in the front seat. Just before Granata arrived, they moved the car to a different spot which was something that should have troubled me more than it did. I told Joe about the car with two antennas but he dismissed it. "Get in the fuckin' car," he said. "You, you're paranoid." I said, "Maybe, but I'm on parole, okay?"

Granata's demeanor was off. He displayed the kind of nervousness that a guy might show when he knows something's about to happen. I told him to follow me to an Oasis further down the toll road but he balked. "No, I don't wanna go nowhere. I'm tired." "Let's get outta here," I said again. "They're not cops," Joe said anxiously. "Let's go inside. Let's go inside." When I told him I'd been watching that car for 15 minutes, he became even more agitated. He said he'd been driving all day and had several more places to go. I still can't believe I let this imbecile talk me out of my gut feeling. Ignoring your gut is almost always a mistake, and in this case it was a doozie.

We went inside and sat down at a table at the Burger King. You can see outside in every direction at an oasis because most of the walls are glass. I saw another car with two antennas move and pointed it out to Granata. I asked him why cops might be tailing him and he told me he couldn't think of a reason. I apparently couldn't think at all and that troubles me to this day.

Granata immediately changed the subject to the guys who were investing in my vehicle flea market. "I bragged about you over there to the older guys," he said. "I told them I got a kid with me now who's gonna make us a lot of money. You'll like 'em. We'll be low key because I don't want you gettin' in no fuckin' trouble because now I'm worried about you." Really? His cousin sent him to kill me, and six months later he was worried about me. We sat for about 15 minutes and I spent almost all of it wondering what the hell was going on. If I had been thinking straight, I would have said to Joe, "Unbutton your shirt." He wouldn't have resisted, and I would have known he was wearing a wire. Unfortunately, I picked a very bad time to be stupid again.

We left the building and walked to our cars. Granata asked me to get into his car so he could give me something. It was cold that day, and I wearing a heavy, quilted parka. I got in the front seat and positioned myself so I could look in several directions and deliver a right hand to Joe's face if necessary. He reached for the athletic bag from under his seat, and put the bag between us. Then, in a separate motion, he placed the bag on my lap. I knew something was wrong and I started to leave the car. I still had one more firewall, and I've asked myself a thousand times why I didn't look in the bag. Had I done that, there would have been no reason to arrest me because that bag would have never left Joe's car. I would have known it was a setup and the ATF's game would have been over. However, my game would have just begun. I would have sued the ATF and the Lake County State's Attorney's office for fraud and malicious prosecution of an innocent man. My case against them would have been all about accountability and they would have paid through the nose in order to keep me from going public with my story. All I needed to do was to look in that damn bag before I exited the car, but I didn't.

As I opened the car door, the bag slid down my leg and onto

the ground and Granata immediately took off. Before the passenger door slammed shut he yelled, "Get the fuck outta here. I hate your fucking guts." Based on that comment alone, I should have left that bag where it dropped, gotten into my car, and driven away. Instead, I unlocked my car door, threw the bag on the floor of the passenger side, and got in.

Imagine a split screen. On the left side is the scene in *Goodfellas* when Henry Hill gets busted in his driveway by a small army of cops and federal agents, all of whom have their guns aimed at him. Hill was a serious mobster. By dealing large amounts of cocaine, he was facing major time in prison unless he flipped on his friends. So he flipped. He gave up important people to avoid going to jail, and then he disappeared into the Witness Protection Program.

On the right side of the screen is a scene similar to the one in *Goodfellas,* only I'm the one being arrested. A small army of cops and ATF agents surrounded me at the Lake Forest Oasis and all of them had their guns pointed at me. Hill and I were both in our cars when it happened, but that's where the similarities ended, because this was no movie. I had been set up by a group of vindictive federal agents, with help from an equally vindictive Lake County assistant state's attorney, all of whom were convinced I was a hitman.

Everything happened in a matter of seconds. A female officer jumped out of a car with her gun drawn and screamed at me, "Get out of the car, motherfucker, and get on your knees." They do shit like this on purpose. The ATF had a woman tell me to get on my knees because they wanted to humiliate me. They handcuffed me behind my back and put me in the backseat of an unmarked car for the 20-minute drive to the Highland Park police station. The driver told me to turn around and pointed out the helicopter above us. I asked him what it was for. "Well, Jack," he said, "you're known for your driving abilities." How they expected me to get out of the parking lot in my own car was something I couldn't quite grasp. No, that helicopter, like everything else about this, was strictly for show and highly personal.

The agents in the car tried to get me to talk about people. They even had the audacity to ask me where Jimmy Hoffa was buried, a question which I completely ignored. But, as long as we're on the subject, here's a message to the Feds: "You can stop digging now."

Before getting booked, I took off my gold bracelet and gold necklace and they put them in an evidence pouch. They put my Seiko watch and $106.85 in cash in separate pouches. One cop joked that I could keep my belt, then asked me to surrender it. It's amazing how brave some cops are when in the presence of an unarmed man who's surrounded by people with loaded guns and hostile intentions.

They took me to an interrogation where James Delorto, Matthew Gorecki and a third ATF agent were waiting for me. They were the same federal agents that had been pursuing me for 13 years, and they had orchestrated this whole thing from the very beginning. Delorto had what I can only describe as a postcoital glow on his face. "Hey Jack," he said with obvious relish, "remember me? How you doing? You gonna talk to us now?" I said, "Why would I talk to you now?" He said, "Because you got a problem here and we can help you make this go away. We have you on tape, Jack." Summoning the kind of pitch-perfect sarcasm I was known for, I said, "Well, I guess you got me."

Delorto's "you gonna talk to us now" question confirmed my suspicions about the ATF's motivation in pursuing me. He was still pissed off at me for not flipping on Dominic and another guy back in 1979, and for lying to the grand jury. It sounds ludicrous, but that doesn't make it any less true. I said, "Why the hell would you go to all this trouble to frame an innocent man? Don't ATF agents have anything better to do?" Delorto flashed a sarcastic little smile, and said. "Excuse me, Mr. Gail, but an innocent man doesn't confess, now does he?" "Confess?" I said. "Confess to what?" Delorto had been recording our conversation and he played back what I had said

20 seconds earlier. I laughed at them when I heard that. Besides, they didn't read me my rights, so anything I said after my arrest couldn't be used against me. "I guess you got me?" Really?

I called Chicago attorney, Dennis Berkson. He knew a lot of the people that I did and he had represented some of them, but I couldn't remember if he got any of them off. Of all the extremely serious errors in judgment that I made that fateful day, hiring Dennis Berkson was by far the worst. It was such a catastrophic mistake that I feel the need to say it again. Of all the extremely serious errors in judgment that I made that fateful day in January, 1992, hiring Dennis Berkson as my attorney was by far the worst. His inadequate defense of me can be attributed to one of three things, and none of them are flattering. Berkson looked and dressed like an attorney, and he acted and sounded like one, too. Of course, in the words of an old Yiddish proverb, "A goat has a beard, but that doesn't make him a rabbi."

I had several witnesses who could have exposed the dishonesty of the State's case, but Berkson refused to call any of them. The state's main witness was a government informant whose cousin wanted me dead, but my attorney never thought that fact was important enough to establish at my trial. I could have proved I was told there would be $100,000 in that gym bag, but Berkson failed to recognize the importance of that, too. He never thought anything I said was important, even though I could refute every single thing in the state's case.

20

HOW DID THINGS EVER GET SO FAR?

MOST OF THE people who ended up working for the Feds were born into middle-class families that looked down on organized crime. James Delorto, Matthew Gorecki, and their peers came of age when the mob was at its weakest. Many of them engaged in personal vendettas against their own nationality and some of them imposed that same vindictiveness on non-Italians like me. They falsified evidence and perjured themselves to satisfy their own personal agendas. They got away with it because the ATF leadership let their agents run roughshod over people's constitutional rights. Other federal law enforcement agencies look down on them.

ATF Special Agents have some of the broadest authority of any federal agency, including lead investigative authority on any federal crime committed with a firearm. They began abusing that authority from the moment they opened their doors in the early 1970's. They have repeatedly engaged in a longstanding pattern of unlawful discrimination and retaliation against private citizens. I read that testimony was submitted to the ATF's Appropriations Subcommittee which claimed that 75% of their gun prosecutions were aimed at ordinary citizens with no criminal intent. Who woulda thunk it?

The ATF routinely ignored federal statutes as well as their own policies. ATF managers, lawyers and agents lied to Congressional committees and other investigative bodies. A Senate subcommittee found the ATF's enforcement tactics to be "constitutionally, legally, and practically, reprehensible," and that was long before their performances at Waco and Ruby Ridge. The illegal conduct of their agents is often rewarded, but it's never censured or even discouraged. They get paid regardless of what they do and regardless of the outcome, and they're often rewarded in other ways for their bad behavior.

Agents spend their days trying to find people who will testify against someone in a court of law. Many ATF agents have no conscience, and it's all one big game to them. If they can't get someone on their own, they'll join forces with local prosecutors to "Tag Team" him. They did that in my case by getting Lake County to help set me up. The ATF ignored the rule of law and they got away with it because local authorities believe everything the Feds tell them. What they say about absolute power is absolutely true. It's what gives Federal agents permission to take the law into their own hands.

When the FBI falsely labelled me a hitman in 1977, it affected me for the rest of my life. Once something goes on your record, it takes on a life of its own. It impacted my family members and my friends, and the ripple effect never ended. Now, if I get introduced to people, the first thing they're going to do is look me up on the Internet to see if I'm the kind of person they want to be around, much less do business with. Before I wrote this book, there wasn't much about me on the Internet but all of it was terrible. If the truth counts for anything at all, that's about to change and it's about fucking time.

Most of my so-called friends never asked me what happened. Many of them probably thought I was guilty and had no desire to find out if what they heard about me was actually true. People still look at me differently after all these years and it's not a good feeling. Whether or not they care, they need to know that the real criminals in my case were the Feds and the Lake County State's Attorney's office. I blame myself to a point because I was stupid at times, but I did nothing criminal.

I spent seven months awaiting trial at the Lake County jail in Waukegan. The cells had a big steel door with a small glass pane so the staff could observe you. The inside of the cell was bare, except for a sink, a toilet, and a small surface that served as a desk or a place to eat. There was an open area in the middle of the facility that allowed guards to view the entire floor. It was better than being in prison but the bullshit in both places is mostly the same.

With a couple of exceptions, everybody treated me fine no matter where I was. I ran into an asshole every now and then but I rarely had a problem with guards. I showed them respect and they reciprocated by treating me like a human being. They liked that I minded my own business and five or six of them told me I'd been set-up. They read the newspaper articles about my case and came to their own conclusions. It's always bothered me that the Feds can engage in a criminal conspiracy to set you up, but it's not a punishable offense for them. Please tell me why it shouldn't be.

The media wanted to believe the worst about me. It's part of the "if it bleeds, it leads" news mentality. They reported that I probably killed a guy so I could move in with his wife, and that I was getting ready to kill another guy who slept with my girlfriend. The ATF and Lake County acted like screenwriters in my case and they tried to come up with a plot line that the jurors would believe. Here's how the Chicago Tribune covered my arraignment.

PAROLEE CHARGED IN MOB DEATH PLOT

A Deerfield man was charged Thursday with solicitation to commit murder for his part in a foiled contract plot to kill an organized crime figure in Florida.

Lake County and federal authorities say the man, Jackie Gail, is an organized crime operative who also is under investigation in connection with the unsolved murder of pizza company executive, Salvatore Canzoneri. Canzoneri was gunned down in his Highland Park home in 1989.

State and federal officials said that Gail is engaged to Canzoneri's widow, Karen.

Local and federal authorities seized Gail at the Lake Forest Oasis of the Tri-State Tollway Tuesday afternoon shortly after he allegedly completed plans with a government operative to murder a mobster in Pompano, Beach, Florida, according to police.

The arrest came after Gail finished discussing the plot with the operative, who was wearing a concealed microphone, authorities said.

Look how they massacred my reputation. By the end of the second paragraph, a lot of readers probably thought I had killed Sam Canzoneri. After reading the next sentence, they were probably convinced that I had. The prosecution treated hearsay as fact, and the media never once questioned it. The fix was definitely in.

21

I GOT THIS

THE PROSECUTION ASKED for a $2,000,000 bond at my arraignment. It seemed a tad high for the crime of picking up a bag whose contents were not what I had been told to expect. I was charged with Unlawful Possession of a Controlled Substance, Unlawful Possession of a Firearm by a Felon, Solicitation to Commit Murder and Armed Violence.

I told the judge, "You can set the bond at $2 and I still can't get out because I'm on parole." When my attorney tried to get me to shut up, I said, "Okay Dennis, just put Ronnie Tortorella, Richie Urso and Gabriel Ponzio on the stand. That's all you have to do because I didn't do any of this." He responded by saying, "This is serious shit here, Jack," as if I didn't know I was facing at least 30 years behind bars if convicted. That was my first inkling that I had hired the wrong attorney.

I told Berkson I wanted to exercise my right to a speedy trial because I didn't want to be involved in this bullshit for any longer than necessary. The right to a speedy trial is guaranteed by the Sixth Amendment to the United States Constitution, and Article 1, Section 8 of the Illinois Constitution. The Speedy Trial Act mandates that an Illinois defendant who remains in custody has the right to be tried within 120 days of his or her arrest. The 120-day period begins automatically and a defendant need do nothing to start the clock ticking. Berkson, however, asked for a continuance without my permission and against my express wishes. That was my second inkling that I had hired the wrong attorney.

The only good reason for an attorney to request a continuance is when the case is so complicated that four months wouldn't give him or her enough time to adequately prepare a defense. The extra time wasn't necessary in my case because I could have laid out the entire story to Berkson in less than an hour if he had been willing to hear me out. There was little need for him to do any research, except for speaking with the witnesses I wanted to testify on my behalf.

I'm not a lawyer, but I should have played one at this trial. I say that because I apparently understood the importance of Criminal Intent better than my attorney did. Criminal Intent is defined as a conscious decision by someone to engage in an unlawful act or to harm another person. It forms the basis for establishing guilt in a criminal case and is a necessary component in prosecuting a crime. What's most important is what's in a person's mind at the time of the crime and what's directing that person's actions.

It would have been easy to prove that I wasn't predisposed to commit any of the criminal offenses of which I was accused. My taped conversations with Granata showed that I ignored his many attempts to get me to partner with him in killing Gabriel Ponzio. I turned down the kilo of cocaine Granata wanted to give me to drop my lien and I declined the 1,800 pounds of hybrid marijuana that he offered to sell me. I refused to take the Uzi that Granata brought me, and did so as forcefully as I could. As far as the 8-ball of cocaine I asked Granata for on January 14, I said, "If you can't get it tonight, forget about it."

I told Granata several times that I didn't want to give law enforcement any reason to look at me. The tapes would have proved that I never said or did anything incriminating, and since the state's entire case against me was based on my conversations with Joe Granata, we needed to listen to those tapes from start to finish. Don't ask me why, but Dennis never asked for a copy of those recordings, even though I asked him to do so on several occasions. The fact that the State was going to play portions of them, entitled me to a complete set of the taped conversations. Since they also played part of Granata's conversations with Gabriel Ponzio, I was entitled to a full set of those conversations as well.

They gave us a transcript of Granata's first conversation with Ponzio. I kept telling Dennis there had to have been a second conversation, and there was. It's when Granata said to Ponzio, "I'll take care of this for you. I'll set him up, and then you'll owe me a favor." That second conversation took place one day after I first met with Granata. Coincidence? I don't think so. Lake County also withheld the tape of the strategy meeting between Joe Granata, April Granata, agent Gorecki and the prosecutors, at which they developed their plan to entice me to meet with Granata under false pretenses at the Lake Forest Oasis.

The ATF had choreographed this thing for six months, and every word out of Granata's mouth was put there by the ATF. My arrest was the very definition of entrapment. They took a confidential informant and used him as their pawn to come after me. My attorney needed to clearly understand what had taken place, so I made a list of the outright lies and holes in the State's case.

1. The prosecution had no probable cause to come after me.

2. The prosecution had no evidence of criminal intent on my part.

3. I never told Granata I wanted to kill Ponzio and I never threatened him.

4. It was Gabriel Ponzio who was attempting to kill me, and that was why I continued to meet with Joe Granata.

5. Joe Granata initiated the contact with me, not visa versa.

6. I never did anything that would incriminate myself during

the six months that I met with Granata. If I had, I would have been immediately arrested and charged.

7. I never suggested to Granata that we commit a crime.

8. I went to Florida twice after meeting Granata and he never knew it. Neither did Gabriel Ponzio.

9. If I had wanted to kill Gabriel Ponzio, why would I move 1,300 miles away from him?

10. If I were a hitman, why would I ask another hitman to help me? Especially a hitman who I already knew was sent to kill me.

11. I expected there to be $100,000 in the gym bag Granata gave me, and Granata's wife, April, could attest to that fact.

12. Almost everything that Granata and Gorecki told the grand jury about me was a lie and I could prove it, point by point.

ATF special agent Matthew Gorecki fabricated his entire Grand Jury testimony. He said Granata cooperated with the ATF in their investigation of me, but the ATF wasn't investigating me for anything. Gorecki claimed that I solicited Granata's help in murdering Gabriel Ponzio, even though they were the ones who sent Granata to me. He said my motive was that Ponzio stole my girlfriend!! Let me be as clear as I possibly can on this issue. Any man who wants to hurt a guy for sleeping with his girlfriend can never really be a man. Nevertheless, that ridiculous statement would form the basis of George Strickland's entire case against me. I never said I wanted to kill Ponzio. Ironically, I had to talk my Chicago and New York friends out of killing him on more than one occasion and it took some convincing to get them to back off.

Gorecki told the Grand Jury that I asked Granata to get me an Uzi to perform the hit on Ponzio. He said Joe was going to take Gabe to a remote area where I would "jump out from behind the bushes and unload my weapon into him." Gorecki painted a "say hello to my little Uzi" picture and I don't know how the room didn't erupt in laughter when he said it. I really don't. Anybody who believed Gorecki's story would have had to be a moron. Maybe being a moron should be a crime. When I didn't touch the Uzi that Granata brought me, that should have been the end of it, but Delorto wouldn't let it go. That was the day the ATF decided to partner with Lake County in ther persecution of me.

Gorecki said I was equipped with a Ruger .357 magnum when I met with Granata at the Oasis, and that also was a lie. I brought no weapon to the Oasis and I had no plans to leave with one. The ATF and Lake County put the gun and the cocaine in the athletic bag before putting it in Granata's car. They knew I was expecting Granata to bring me $100,000 and some Frank Sinatra cassettes because that's what they told Granata's wife to tell me when she called me the previous day.

After I was indicted, I realized that the prosecution intended to use my sarcasm as evidence of criminal intent. Delorto told me as much when he replayed my, "Well, I guess you got me" comment. I said a lot of tough guy shit to Granata, and the prosecution was going to use it to establish the worthlessness of my character. I needed my attorney to point out that the ATF's so-called investigation of me was actually a calculated setup.

I should have walked at my pre-trial hearing because they had no probable cause. If Dennis Berkson had taken the time to hear my side of the story, he could have compared the prosecution's case to a house of cards built on sand. The ATF decided to pursue me only after my name got mentioned on a phone conversation between two organized crime figures, one of whom was a longtime informant for the federal government, and the other one was a woman beater. I told Berkson to challenge the prosecution on probable cause, but he wouldn't do it. "Don't worry about it," he said. "I got this." He actually said that to me, over and over and over again.

Berkson could and should have challenged everything Gorecki

said at that hearing but he shut me down every time I tried to tell him what to do. There were questions that the ATF should have been forced to answer, but my attorney was afraid to challenge the court. I said, "Dennis, why don't you object?" He dismissed my question and said, "Just leave it alone, Jack." That was inkling number three that I should have gotten a new attorney.

The prosecution was forced to convene a second preliminary hearing to notify the court that their star witness, Joe Granata, was put into Witness Protection after informing on a major Chicago crime figure and his crew. You'd think this would have given my defense team a little leverage, but they didn't recognize the opportunity. Delorto took the stand and was asked the same questions that had been asked of Gorecki, and he reiterated his partner's lies. Berkson didn't challenge anything Delorto said, just like he never challenged anything throughout this entire process. I said, "Dennis, why aren't you questioning Delorto?" and he said, "Jack, I got this." That's all my attorney ever said to me. I told him there was no probable cause, and he said, "I got this." I said there was no criminal intent, and he said, "I got this." I told him Delorto was lying through his teeth and he said, "I got this."

My arrest should never have been anything more than an expensive and gross waste of time. I have no doubt that a first-year law student could have walked me right out of court, because the prosecution literally had nothing to justify my arrest, much less my conviction. They said I had contacted Granata to help me kill Ponzio and they used that lie as the basis for their probable cause. But at some point they would have had to explain who sent Joe Granata to me and for what reason.

Agent Gorecki needed to be asked a series of damning questions from my legal team that would have been difficult for him to answer, given his previous statements and actions. The most important question was why didn't the ATF tell me that my son was in danger and why wasn't Gabriel Ponzio arrested for threatening to kidnap him?

What motivated their investigation of me in the first place and when did it start? What probable cause did the ATF have to justify pursuing me? How much taxpayer money was spent on setting me up? Who approved this ATF operation and who told Granata to lie? Those and many other questions were germane to these proceedings. Any defense attorney worth his salt would have relished the opportunity to call bullshit on a federal agency that violated the rule of law as blatantly and as often as the ATF did. Hell, I could have won this case if I had represented myself, and I wish to God that I had.

22

FEDERAL WITHHOLDING

THE DISCOVERY PROCESS requires the disclosure of all relevant facts and documents to the defendant prior to trial. The language is quite clear on this matter. Any party has a right to see most documents that even marginally impact their case. It's part of that whole innocent until proven guilty concept. In their Disclosure to the Accused, the State said I would be provided with the following things. My comments are in parentheses.

1. Any relevant written or recorded statements of the witnesses, and any memoranda containing substantially verbatim reports of any oral statements.

(Relevant statements? Substantially verbatim reports? Just give me the damn evidence, please!)

2. All statements of the defendant, and any memoranda of the substance of any oral statements of the defendant.

(All statements, my ass! Giving us the "substance" of my conversations with Granata was like using Cliff Notes to write a book review on War and Peace. They cut and pasted my sarcastic comments and used them to establish criminal intent.)

3. A transcript of the Grand Jury proceedings.

(If they provided that to my attorney, and I don't know that they did, he never asked me about it, and he apparently never read it.)

4. Any prior record of criminal convictions which may be used for impeachment of the State's witnesses at hearing or at trial.

(The State gave us a carefully edited summary of Granata's involvement with the ATF. They refused to provide us with agreements between Granata and any federal law enforcement agency, even though he had worked for four of them in the past 10 years, and was paid more than $30,000 a year in salary and bonuses. They also refused to tell us whether Granata avoided criminal prosecution as a result of his cooperation.)

5. All exhibits currently available may be inspected by the defendant and his attorney at a time to be agreed upon following reasonable notice to Assistant State's Attorneys Strickland or Kornak.

(Not only were they hiding evidence from the defense, they were going to make it as inconvenient as possible to look at that which they were permitting me to see. Thanks to my attorney, I never got to see any of it, except for the transcript of Granata's first conversation with Ponzio, when I first learned he had planned to kidnap my son.)

6. Any prior record of criminal convictions which may be used for impeachment of the State's witnesses at hearing or trial are attached. Further records will be forthcoming.

(Further records would be provided when hell froze over. No witness was ever more impeachable than Joe Granata and a look at his criminal record would have exposed his total lack of credibility and integrity.)

7. There has been no electronic surveillance in this case.

(George Strickland was nothing, if not dishonest. He lied, despite the fact that every one of my conversations with Joe Granata had been recorded. Just because it was the ATF that made the recordings, doesn't mean he didn't have them. After denying there was any electronic surveillance, he turned around and played those portions of the recordings which they believed would strengthen their case.)

If you read between the lines, the prosecutors were saying I'd only get what *they* considered to be evidence, not the evidence itself. Their overriding strategy was to deny me the ability to mount an effective defense. Lake County denied me due process, and I still can't understand how Dennis Berkson let them get away it. Due process is guaranteed by Amendments Five, Six and Fourteen of the U.S. Constitution, which obligates the State to turn over all materials to a defendant that tend to negate guilt.

When Dennis came to see me in jail for the first time, I tried to explain what led to my arrest. We hadn't talked about my case on the phone and I wanted to make sure we were on the same page. It was obvious that he didn't want to be there and he didn't want to talk about my case, either. He told me to be quiet because the place was bugged. I said, "Dennis, you need to know what happened here and you don't want to hear it." He said, "Jack, you'll be fine. I got this." I said, "Are you crazy? You need to hear the story and I need you to get Ronnie Tortorella, Gabriel Ponzio, Richie Urso and April Granata on the stand." It was as if I were speaking a foreign language of which he was totally unfamiliar.

Berkson came to see me on six occasions when I was awaiting trial and never stayed longer than 20 minutes. He was always in a hurry, always in a rush. He acted like it was an imposition for him to drive the 45 minutes from downtown Chicago to talk to me, despite the fact that he was getting paid to do it. "Jack," he'd say, "you didn't do anything wrong so don't worry about it. I got this." A word to the wise: In the event you ever meet me, the only time I want to hear the words "I got this," is if you're picking up the check.

Dennis Berkson must have thought I was either stupid or guilty, or maybe he had another agenda of which I was unaware. Correct me if I'm wrong, but wouldn't any capable defense attorney want to hear his client's side of the story? Wouldn't he have an obligation to do that? Wouldn't an attorney want all the facts at his disposal before deciding on a strategy? That bullshit about the room being bugged actually scared me because I couldn't imagine why any attorney would even bring that up.

I couldn't mount an effective defense without meeting with my legal team, so what's the point of having an attorney if I couldn't talk to him? If there wasn't a place where I could speak privately with Berkson, then Berkson should have screamed bloody murder until one was made available. I also couldn't defend myself without having access to everything I was entitled to receive in the Discovery Process, and Dennis never asked for most of it. A life-size cardboard cutout of a lawyer would have been a lot cheaper and would have provided the same level of legal representation that I received from Dennis Berkson.

Our first motion was to suppress my so-called confession, something which should have been raised at my pre-trial hearing. If you heard the tape of me saying, "Well, I guess you got me," you'd know I was being sarcastic. It's a cliche, for Christ sake! Even if I were sincere when I said it, the statement couldn't have been used against me because I didn't voluntarily waive my right to counsel, nor did I waive my right to remain silent.

Murderers, rapists and child molesters have walked free because they weren't read their Miranda rights at the time of their arrest. Every rookie cop is told that you don't question a suspect without first reading him his rights. They actually carry the 55-word statement in their shirt pockets to make sure they say it exactly as it's written. So how did Gorecki get around it? He said he didn't Mirandize me because I knew he and Delorto were ATF agents. Judge Raymond McKoski found that reasoning compelling enough to dismiss my motion. I apparently was the exception to several law enforcement rules, because this was indicative of the way I was treated throughout this ordeal.

Granata's substantial criminal record and his years as a government informant were withheld from me and the court. The truth was that he betrayed people for a living and all he had to do to stay out of prison was to sell his soul. By this point in his life, I doubt that he still had one. Once the jury knew that Granata was on the payroll of his fourth different federal agency as a rat, and that he was paid handsomely for his "cooperation," they would have questioned his truthfulness. The ATF and Lake County knew that better than anyone, so they denied me access to his file.

Another thing they withheld about Granata was the testimony of ATF agent, Daniel Ivancich. He came to the ATF in January, 1991, after working as an agent of the Department of Agriculture for two-and-a-half years. Granata was the first informant he had ever worked with and Ivancich was assigned to Joe when the ATF was setting up a major Outfit guy who I'll call Mr. X. The following interview took place a couple of months before Granata was ordered by Delorto to set me up.

> *DI: This was my first purchase of weapons. I was present for a meeting between Mr. Granata and Mr. X.*
>
> *ATF: Was this conversation on November 17 before or after the agents learned of the unauthorized, unrecorded, unsurveilled alleged purchase of cocaine from Mr. X by Mr. Granata?*
>
> *DI: He bought the machine guns and another firearm from Mr. X prior to that.*
>
> *ATF: Once you learned about the unauthorized purchase, wouldn't that have caused you some concern, this indication on the tape, which was Mr. Granata saying the night before he bought the guns he was up all night doing cocaine with the Puerto Ricans?*
>
> *DI: When Mr. Granata was confronted about it, he admitted that he did that.*
>
> *ATF: You didn't interrogate him, though, correct?*
>
> *DI: No. I didn't prepare any report, but I had talked to him.*

ATF: Did Mr. Granata have any type of a record or file with DEA that you were aware of?

DI: No, I am not.

ATF: Were you ever made aware of, or told that Mr. Granata had previously been institutionalized — by "previously" I mean prior to this investigation — in a mental institution.

DI: No, sir.

ATF: You'd never been told that?

DI: No sir.

Allow me to summarize. The prosecution's main witness against me was a hitman who was emotionally disturbed and addicted to hard drugs. Rather than keeping his nose clean, Granata was doing his own gun and cocaine deals on the side, and suffered no consequences because of it. Granata clearly knew how to work the federal system and the ATF turned a blind eye to his extracurricular activities.

There was another interview that would have been a problem for the prosecution. On March 10, 1992, Gabriel Ponzio was interviewed by ATF Special Agents Pamela J. Durham and Lazara Gomila. He was asked about his relationship with me and he said he never had one. He told the agents he had dated Sophia Sokorski on and off for the last 21 years. In the mid-1980s, he broke up with her and moved to Chicago. When Ponzio returned to Florida a year later, he secretly re-established his relationship with Sophia while she was living with me. Ponzio said I showed no reaction to the break-up and that I never tried to contact either of them at any time. He said he was never threatened by me and could think of no reason why I would want him killed.

There were so many provable lies in the prosecution's case that the Federal courts would have never signed off on an operation like this. Nothing I did warranted their relentless pursuit, and that's why they sought Lake County's help in framing me.

Lake County prosecutors violated the very nature of the equal protection clause of the Constitution of the United States and the State of Illinois. Withholding crucial evidence that goes to the guilt or innocence of a defendant violates the most basic requirements of due process. It's what lawyers call Hiding the Weenie. Making up evidence is even more egregious and the ATF and Lake County did both of those things. They did it in such an obvious way that I couldn't understand how my attorney let them get away with that.

Delorto and Gorecki told Lake County I was a hitman and a major player in organized crime in both Ft. Lauderdale and Chicago. They sweetened the deal by telling them that one of my probable victims was a Highland Park resident whose gangland-style murder had never been solved. It's as if this were a play, based on an original story by the FBI and the U.S. Attorney's office, written by Matthew Gorecki, directed by James Delorto, and produced by the Bureau of Alcohol, Tobacco and Firearms.

Imagine being on a Hollywood studio lot. Those buildings you see look real, but they're not. No one really cares if the buildings are genuine as long as they provide credibility for a story on which everyone is trying to get the audience to believe. Lake County, with considerable help from the ATF, engaged in a similar kind of misdirection to get the jurors to focus solely on their story, and my attorney was kind enough to let them. By making up a scenario about who I was and what I was supposedly planning to do, the behavior of the prosecutors wasn't much different than the way studio executives get people to buy into the premise of their movies.

The conspiracy against me was particularly outrageous and mean-spirited in that it had its genesis in a death threat against me, a fact I could have established in 15 minutes with the testimony of two witnesses. All Dennis Berkson had to do was to subpoena them, but he didn't! The question is why, and I don't have the answer. Part of the problem is that judges, prosecutors and defense attorneys attend the same charity events, frequent the same restaurants, and their kids go to the same schools. No matter which side they're on, the attorneys are all part of a club and they're always incredibly polite to each other, no matter what's at stake. Sometimes they stick to the truth but most of their time is spent trying to outwit each other and to fool the jury. That's especially true when the facts of the case are not in their favor. Winning often depends on who knows the most tricks or who has the most stature, but it should always depend on the truth, the whole truth, and nothing but the truth. Attorneys all play the game the same way and, unfortunately, that's what lawyering has become in this country.

I was told a long time ago that only 10% of lawyers are worth their salt and federal agents know that better than anyone. Most attorneys come from comfortable families and are encouraged by their parents to practice law in order to make a good living. They act like they're part of an elite fraternity that doesn't want clients interfering with their business. Of course, that's a contradiction in terms because your business *is* their business once you pay them. Your business is the reason they're *in* business in the first place. For some reason, Dennis Berkson thought he could conduct *his* business without knowing very much about me. I asked him to hold a mock trial and he actually laughed. "Get out of here," he said, "we don't need a mock trial." Throughout the run-up to the trial, he arrogantly dismissed everything that I thought was crucial to a winning defense, beginning with the only thing that really mattered - the facts.

23

A STACKED DECK

JOE GRANATA CAME to court looking absolutely ridiculous. His head was shaved and he had grown a mustache and beard that were dyed black. He was heavily guarded by U.S. marshals, and, in an unprecedented move, an armed marshal stood directly behind him while he testified. The inference, of course, was that he needed protection but was too brave a man not to testify. It's interesting that Granata had never been required to testify in any of the cases he helped the government make in his capacity as a Confidential Informant, because the taped evidence spoke for itself. In my case, it didn't.

Granata admitted he worked for the mob while he was ratting on them, but claimed he changed his career in 1990 when a former high school buddy who was a Treasury agent got him a job as a CI. George Strickland wanted the jury to believe that Granata cooperated with the ATF because he had finally seen the light. The fictionalized account of his "How I came to Jesus" moment was put forth as a triumph of good over evil. But make no mistake, the only reason a criminal becomes a CI is to avoid serving jail time, and that was Granata's motivation. To assert otherwise is strictly bullshit, and it's startling to realize the lengths the ATF and Lake County went to in order to set me up.

At most criminal trials, attorneys treat their clients like they don't matter. The defendant sits there like a pawn on a chess board because everything is out of his hands and in the hands of the lawyers. My defense team suggested I try to look studious by pretending to take notes, which I opted not to do.

The atmosphere in the courtroom wasn't negative, except for the humiliation I felt over Strickland's insistence that I wanted to kill a guy for sleeping with my girlfriend. The animosity with which Strickland presented the case was apparent in every question he asked of his only three witnesses, Joe Granata, Matthew Gorecki and James Delorto.

Whenever Delorto looked at me, his face dripped with venom and if he had actually spoken, he would have said, "I got you now, motherfucker." I've been told that some Feds just have a thing for certain people, and for whatever reason, they don't like them. If they think they can get them, they'll do whatever is necessary. They have no conscience. Once federal agents make it personal, anything goes, and this case was strictly personal to Delorto and everyone else involved in setting me up.

It's difficult to overstate the viciousness with which the ATF came at me. Gorecki's job was to corroborate the lies of his pawn, which was easy to do because he was the guy who made up Granata's lies in the first place. Joe testified for less than 30 minutes, and most of his time was spent responding to the prosecutor's questions, rather than the few asked by Dennis Berkson. Every time my attorney objected to the State's questions, the objections were overruled. Every time he asked a question of Granata, the prosecution objected, and all of their objections were sustained. What made it worse was that Berkson wasn't even asking the right questions.

The prosecution played the portions of the tapes where I was being sarcastic because those were the only words I spoke that *might* have been construed as incriminating, provided you didn't hear the conversation in its entirety. Taken on face value, my words were damning because those were the only words that the jury was allowed to hear. Sarcasm is situational and obvious when you hear it in context, but you need context to actually recognize it. It doesn't necessarily reveal itself in print, either.

When Granata said he liked to see people suffer before he killed them, I had responded by saying, 'Well I don't. Does that give you a hard-on, Joe?" To the prosecution, "Well, I don't," was proof that I was a hitman. They also played the parts of the tapes when I said, "Can you get me an Uzi," "My face will be the last thing he sees," and, "Well, I guess you got me." Strickland used my sarcasm like it was DNA in order to establish a motive for me wanting to kill Ponzio. That was all they had on me after six long months, which means they had absolutely nothing.

The recordings would have proven my innocence, rather than my guilt, and it wasn't a close call. The only thing on those tapes that could have gotten me into trouble was my sarcasm, and that's what eventually did. If Berkson had demanded a copy of those recordings from the prosecution, He could have shown that nothing else on the tapes even hinted that I wanted to commit any crime, much less murder.

Strickland was as serious as a heart attack. His job was to get 12 jurors to believe that I wanted to kill Gabriel Ponzio because he slept with my girlfriend. "In the world of La Cosa Nostra," he said, "any reason to kill a guy is a good reason." (Good thing I didn't wear my leather *La Cosa Nostra* club jacket to the trial.) Strickland's premise was an easy thing to disprove but my attorney never even tried. The prosecution ignored Ponzio's threat to kidnap my son, and my attorney never brought that up either. His trial strategy consisted almost solely of going after Granata's character, rather than proving my innocence. He said he was going to "shove Granata's testimony up his ass." What the hell does that even mean? In point of fact, Berkson didn't refute a single thing that Granata said, and everything Granata said was a lie. Everything!

Prior to my trial, Granata had been instructed on several

occasions not to make any reference to my being on parole. The court did that because the prosecution isn't allowed to introduce prior past deeds of the defendant at a trial unless the defendant or his attorney brings it up. If the prosecution brings it up, it provides a defendant with grounds for a mistrial or an appeal. During Granata's cross-examination by my attorney, the following exchange took place:

Q. Mr. Gail didn't go down to Florida with you in December on the 28th, did he?

A. No, he didn't.

Q. He went without you, correct?

A. (Nodding head.)

Q. Isn't that true?

A. Must be.

Q. Okay. And you weren't down in Florida in December of 1991, were you, sir?

A. No. No, but his probation officer knew.

When Berkson asked the court to strike Granata's remark, the judge asked the jurors to raise their hands if they couldn't disregard his comment, and none of them did. Then he ordered a brief recess so he could question Granata in his chambers. After a couple of minutes, Joe admitted he did it on purpose. The judge told him not to make any similar remarks in the future, as if that would erase what the jury had already heard.

The jury now knew I had a criminal past, even if they didn't know the specifics. That meant my silence on this matter no longer made sense. If I testified, my previous conviction would be an obstacle for me to overcome, but that didn't change the underlying facts of this case, and the facts were on my side. I told Berkson I wanted to testify on my own behalf and he said, "Jack, if you want to do that, get yourself another attorney!" He didn't say that in jest. He was actually prepared to walk out on me in the middle of the trial.

If I were prone to violence, that comment by my attorney would have triggered it. I'd already paid him a lot of money but he threatened to quit the case because I wanted to have a say in my own defense. Given the attorney-client privilege, I kind of assumed that I didn't need to worry about my attorney betraying me, but I was wrong. Berkson seemed intent on losing this case on his own, with no help from me. I knew what I would have been exposing myself to had I testified, but I needed to present the defense that my attorney never did.

Berkson's ultimatum put me between a rock and a bigger rock. I knew how bad it would look if I changed attorneys at the last minute, no matter how valid my reasons were. Most likely the jurors would have seen a drowning man flailing his arms in an attempt to keep his head above water. Short of Berkson keeling over in court, which would have triggered a mistrial, I felt my only option was to testify on my own behalf or deliver my own closing argument.

If this were a personal injury case and the defense made me a financial offer, my attorney would have told them it was his client's decision to accept or reject the offer and he'd get back to them. Anything else would have been malpractice. When 30 years of my life were on the line, it was even more important for me to make the final decisions. Rather than look at this from my point of view, which was the only view that mattered, Dennis Berkson threw a hissy fit and threatened to withdraw from the trial.

Berkson either never understood, or didn't want to understand that proving Lake County and the ATF set me up should have been the basis of my defense. The reason for that strategy was simple, because it was the truth. The only crime that was committed was the conspiracy that was perpetrated against me. Matthew Gorecki was an ATF special agent who perjured himself by lying under oath. The cross-examination of him should have been rigorous, but Berkson didn't question him at all.

My fate was in Dennis Berkson's hands, and that meant I was doomed. I'm not making this up, but he put my accountant on the stand to talk about the cost and income analysis he had prepared for my vehicle flea market. AS MY ONLY FUCKING WITNESS! I had to stay calm, which wasn't easy for me to do at that moment in time. I said, "Wait a minute fellas, this doesn't seem logical," and was promptly ignored. Berkson thought the testimony of a guy who had nothing to do with the case, and nothing to offer in my defense, was the way to rebut the prosecutor's claim that I wanted to kill Gabriel Ponzio, a crime for which I wasn't even on trial.

Why didn't he put April Granata on the stand? She would have testified, under penalty of perjury, that she called me the day before my arrest to tell me that Joe would be bringing me $100,000 and some Frank Sinatra cassettes with him to our meeting. Or what about putting Ronnie Tortorella on the stand to prove that the guy I supposedly wanted to murder had actually solicited his help in a plot to murder me.

Even better, why not put Richie Urso on the stand. By calling Richie as a witness, we could have pinpointed the very beginning of the ATF's criminal conspiracy against me. We would have established that the ATF agents initiated the contact between Granata and me, rather than what they said under oath. Richie would have been asked to name the agent who ordered him to give me Granata's phone number, and I strongly suspect he would have said the name James Delorto.

Getting a copy of my taped conversations with Granata, and playing them in their entirety for the jury to hear, would have been helpful. The Jack Gail heard on those recordings never mentioned murder, or wanting to deal drugs, or do anything illegal. The only so-called evidence of my criminal intent came from Granata's written recollection of our October 10 meeting when the ATF's listening device supposedly failed to record a single word. Coincidence? I don't think so. Granata was incapable of speaking in complete sentences, much less writing a cogent statement. The jury probably would have wondered if Granata could write at all, but, like I said, Dennis never asked for the tapes.

You didn't need a law degree to defend me. What you needed was an ability to think logically and a willingness to confront authority. I would have been better off getting my representation from a public defender because he or she would have listened to me. My case could have been a reputation builder for a young attorney because of the ease by which they could have gotten me off.

During the trial, Berkson made no attempt to contradict the perjured testimony of Granata, which he could have done if he had put my witnesses on the stand. Instead, Berkson talked about the arson Granata had committed and wondered out loud if he thought he was renovating the neighborhood by setting the fire. I didn't know whether to laugh or cry. My attorney acted like a comedian and he seemed better suited for that vocation than he did for the practice of law. Rather than scoring points with the jury, he tried to make them laugh, and I had to sit there and keep my mouth shut.

"The issue in this case is whether Jack Gail had knowledge of what was in that bag," said Berkson. "Jack thought it was money." That was true, and Dennis could have proved that if he had subpoenaed April Granata to testify, which he didn't. Berkson told the jury that I didn't commit armed violence based on an Illinois conviction which was overturned in court. It was as if he had heard something to that effect, rather than having researched the matter, because that was all he said about it.

That was the entirety of Berkson's closing argument and it presented a tiny problem for me. The basis for Lake County's armed violence charge was their insistence that I had intended to kill Gabriel Ponzio, high on an 8-ball of cocaine, and that I planned to do it with the gun that they put in that athletic bag. My defense should have been focussed on undermining that bogus claim, but

Berkson never brought it up. How is that even possible? Twenty seven years later, I still don't know.

What I do know is that it was unconstitutional to convict me of armed violence, because my predicate offense didn't allow for its imposition. I was initially charged with solicitation to commit murder, armed violence and having a controlled substance while in possession of a Class 2 weapon. Lake County then separated the solicitation charge, ostensibly so they could try me for that at a later date. Whatever their reason, they actually hurt their case for armed violence by doing that.

In 1970, the Illinois General Assembly passed the Armed Violence statute. The legislature adopted the law to impose a greater penalty when a firearm was used or discharged in the commission of a crime, as opposed to the use of less-lethal weapons, and it carried a maximum sentence of 30 years. The statute effectively increased the penalty for violent crimes by having the sentence for armed violence run consecutively, rather than concurrently, with the sentence for the predicate offenses of solicitation to commit murder and solicitation of murder for hire.

By removing the predicate offense of solicitation to commit murder, Lake County's charge of armed violence rested on the predicate offense of possession of a controlled substance. Since that crime carried a minimal sentence, armed violence wasn't an appropriate charge in my case. Using it against me was unconstitutional, something of which many attorneys whose clients were charged with armed violence seemed to have been aware. I'll give you a few examples.

Daniel Lombardi was arrested for selling a controlled substance to an undercover police officer while carrying a handgun in his jacket pocket. He was indicted on one count of armed violence, which was predicated on the felony of possession and sale of a controlled substance while armed with a Class 1 weapon. Prior to the trial, Lombardi's attorney moved to dismiss the armed violence count because it violated the Proportionate Penalties clause of both the Illinois and U.S. Constitutions.

Another man, Elijah Thomas, was charged with possession of a controlled substance, unlawful use of a weapon and armed violence. Like Lombardi, his attorney filed a pretrial motion to dismiss the armed violence charge, which was predicated on possession of a controlled substance while armed with a Class 1 weapon. Thomas's attorney asserted that the penalty would have been unconstitutionally disproportionate to the crime.

Shavez Evans and Timothy Washing committed residential burglary while armed with a handgun, and were also charged with armed violence. Prior to their trials, their attorneys moved to dismiss the armed violence charge by arguing that although their predicate offense was nonviolent, it might have resulted in a greater penalty than that for violent crimes such as home invasion.

The attorneys for Lombardi, Thomas, Evans and Washing maintained that based on the facts of their cases, there wasn't a proper predicate felony for armed violence and that their client's constitutional guarantees of due process and proportionate penalties had been violated. The circuit court agreed and dismissed the armed violence charges against all four men. Unlike me, all four men were arrested while committing a crime. My crime was taking possession of a bag without looking to see what was inside of it, and I didn't hurt anybody but myself by doing it. Ironically, I'm the only one of the five who got convicted of armed violence, and the only one who even went to trial for it. All of this begs the question: Why didn't Dennis Berkson do the same thing for me that those four attorneys did for their clients?

24

THE DEFENSE SLEEPS

WHEN MY ATTORNEY was about to say the defense rests, I told myself to get up and tell the judge I wanted to address the court. After he dismissed the jury, I would have said the following:

"Your honor, I don't know what trial my attorney is attending, because it's not the one going on here. Mr. Berkson told me if I wanted to testify, I'd need to get a new attorney. Whether or not his behavior is unethical is not why I'm bringing this up. Mr. Berkson thinks I shouldn't testify on my own behalf because I have a prior conviction. Of course, because of Joe Granata's intentional slip of the tongue, the jury already knows that.

"The only reason I'm here today is because ATF Special Agent James Delorto heard my name mentioned on a recorded phone conversation between his confidential informant, Joe Granata, and Gabriel Ponzio, a man who wanted to kill me. Neither Ponzio nor Granata knew me, but agent Delorto did. I wasn't under investigation for any crime, nor had I been since being paroled eight years earlier. He heard Mr. Ponzio tell Mr. Granata that he might need him to kidnap my son in order to get me to drop a lien on a house in which he had no legal or financial interest. Nevertheless, the only thing agent Delorto cared about in this conversation was me.

"Agent Delorto had a moral and ethical responsibility to inform me of the threat against my son, but he didn't, and my attorney let him get away with it. The decision by the ATF, the U.S. attorneys and Lake County prosecutors not to tell me that my son was in danger is unforgivable and reprehensible. There was absolutely nothing to connect me to any crime or criminal activity, but agent Delorto willfully ignored the threats against me and my son in order to pursue his own mean-spirited, personal agenda. Your honor, justice may be blind, but injustice has 20/20 vision.

"Because of Granata's intentional slip of the tongue, my attorney's formerly sage advice about my testifying is now a debatable issue. I believe the final decision on whether I should testify on my own behalf is mine to make. I need to conduct my own defense because Dennis Berkson never presented one, and he knows it. He can leave right now, or he can stay and fulfill his obligation to me and the court. By allowing me one additional day to present my defense, I'm confident the evidence I'll present will create enough reasonable doubt to result in an acquittal. If you'll allow me to list the things in my defense that my attorney somehow failed to recognize as important, I believe you'll understand why I'm making this request.

"The prosecution subverted the Discovery Process by withholding the transcripts of my conversations with Joe Granata, as well as the actual tape recordings. They used parts of them in this trial, but they never afforded me that same opportunity. The transcript of the October 10, 1991 conversation was entirely fabricated. Agent Gorecki said he got Granata to write down his recollections, recollections which would provide, among other things, the so-called evidence of my wanting to kill Gabriel Ponzio. Everything in Granata's statement was a lie and I can prove it.

"The fact that Lake County denied me the tapes and transcripts of my conversations with Joe Granata is, I believe, proof of Mr. Strickland's complicity in a scheme hatched by the ATF. Strickland listened to the tapes and he read the transcripts. Then he ignored them, just like the ATF knew he would. Like James Delorto and Matthew Gorecki, George Strickland turned a blind eye to the explicit threat of violence made against my son. He was praying that nobody would bring it up and my attorney was kind enough to oblige him.

"ATF special agent James Delorto had a personal beef with me so he found a prosecutor in George Strickland who also has a personal beef with me. Mr. Strickland wants to think I was involved in the Sam Canzoneri murder even though there's no evidence to support his claim. That's why Mr. Strickland enthusiastically joined forces with the ATF. In Strickland's mind, everything lines up perfectly against me. Guy meets girl. Guy wants girl. Girl is married. Guy kills girl's husband. Some minds work that way but it's not the way the business of justice should work. You don't get to make up facts or treat assumptions as truth, but Mr. Strickland has done both.

"There's one final thing, your honor. I may be the only one in this courtroom to recognize that George Strickland is one hell of a magician. I'm on trial for armed violence but the case he just presented to the jury and this court was for solicitation to commit murder. He intends to try me for that crime two months from now, and he'll present the same case that he just did. The reason George Strickland didn't present a case for armed violence, the crime for which I'm on trial, is because he couldn't win that case. He didn't have probable cause, so he manufactured it, and my attorney let him get away with it. If I'm allowed one additional day to present my defense, I'll talk about the things I've just said in greater detail and produce the witnesses that will establish my innocence. Thank you for giving me the opportunity to speak." I'm pretty sure the judge would have granted my request.

Meanwhile, back in the real world, the prosecution laid it on real thick. "The defendant knew exactly what was going on that day," Assistant State's Attorney Kornak said in his summation to the jury. "The motive for the gun was to kill Gabriel Ponzio. The motive for the cocaine was that Jack Gail wanted it for his personal consumption when he went to Las Vegas."

Then George Strickland made his closing argument. He was

allowed to show the jury the gym bag that Granata placed on my lap, as well as the unloaded .357 magnum and the cocaine that they put with it. At Paul Manafort's first trial, the prosecution talked about the wildly expensive, weird clothes he bought with his laundered money and wanted to show the items to the jury. The judge said it would have been prejudicial and wouldn't allow them to do it. I'm sure the jurors would have gotten a kick out of touching a piece of clothing that nobody had ever seen before, but it wouldn't have influenced their thinking when they began to deliberate Manafort's fate.

Almost every juror was afraid of handling such a powerful gun, even though they knew it was unloaded, just like it was when the ATF put it in that athletic bag. There was nothing proper about any of this but my attorney was mute. "Jack Gail clearly asked for these things," said Strickland. "This business in Itasca had nothing to do with cocaine or an Uzi and the killing of Gabriel Ponzio." Then, Strickland pointed his finger at me and told the jury, "Had Jack Gail not been arrested on January 28, Gabriel Ponzio would be dead today!" With that statement, the State rested its case against me.

About six hours into their deliberations, the jury notified the judge that they wanted to hear the actual tape recordings. I was walked back to court through the tunnel that connected the courthouse to the Lake County jail. If Strickland was worried, he needn't have been. Judge McKoski denied their request by saying the tapes weren't evidence, but the transcripts were. "The jury's deliberative process has already lasted a considerable amount of time," he added. Correct me if I'm wrong, but I don't believe there's a time limit on jury deliberations. I'm also quite certain that the spoken word is a lot more reliable than someone's interpretation of it.

The ruling made no sense, and that's what I told Berkson. The judge's position was comparable to Rudy Giuliani saying, "The truth isn't the truth," but my attorney didn't raise a single objection. Instead, Dennis Berkson drew upon his years of legal training and knowledge and said, "Take it easy, Jack, calm down. It's ok, I got this." It's a funny thing, but I've noticed that my fists ball up everytime I think about that.

I was taken back to Lake County Jail to await the verdict. A couple of inmates asked me about the trial but most of them had as much interest in my case as their dogs did. That's just the way it is. During my first incarceration, a guy told me, "Jack, nobody cares." Come on, I said to myself, people have to care, but he was right. Nobody cares, and that evidently included my attorney.

It was 8:30 pm when the sergeant walked me back to court for the verdict. "You know Jack," he said, "the jury has been out for nine hours and you may just beat this case." Like I said before, six different corrections officers told me they heard I was set up. You can never stop people from talking and cops and guards talk just like everyone else. For the record, I told the guard I wasn't beating anything. How could I, when my attorney failed to present a defense?

When I got back to court, Berkson's usual cocksure smile was on his face but his eyes told me he knew I was going to lose. Strickland was all business, but the malice in Delorto's face was unmistakable and undiluted. Sure enough, the jury found me guilty. The only question that remained was how much time I was going to get.

At the sentencing hearing six weeks later, Strickland lobbied for the full 30 years and was allowed to introduce hearsay evidence. It sounds illegal, but it's not. Lake County produced a number of the agents who had been present at my arrest, and they said I was an important and influential member of La Cosa Nostra. They spoke the name as if each syllable was a word in itself. "La-Co-sa-Nos-tra." They even tried to say the words with an Italian accent.

Strickland double-downed on the perjured testimony of Gorecki and Granata. He claimed I wanted Granata to help me set up an Illinois-to-Florida drug pipeline which was just one of the schemes to which Granata tried to get me to commit. Using my sarcasm against me, he insisted I had discussed the ways I killed people. Strickland conceded there was no evidence of prior killings, nor did he mention the names of who I was supposed to have killed. He asserted that the court had already heard "fairly substantial evidence" that killing Ponzio was my ultimate goal. That evidence never existed and he knew it, but he didn't care. As far as Strickland was concerned, the truth was whatever he said it was, and if my attorney cared to refute it, he should have done it.

The press coverage was predictably brutal. The media wanted to believe the worst about me because, in their minds, it made for a better story. The Chicago Tribune printed the following report on the sentencing hearing:

Mob Tapes: I Never Let Anybody Beg.

As Jack Gail and Joseph Granata drank coffee in a Rosemont restaurant last December, they talked privately of their experiences as killers, according to secret tape recordings.

Granata, 51. a former Chicago mob enforcer turned government informant, said he liked to see his victims plead for their lives.

"No, I never let anybody beg," responded Gail, according to a recording of the conversation that was entered into court proceedings in Lake County on Tuesday.

Lake County Assistant State's Attorneys George Strickland and John Kornak say the tapes prove Gail's propensity for crime, and they asked Circuit Court Judge Raymond McKoski to consider the tapes when he sentences Gail on Thursday.

"What we are basically trying to do is show what they were going to do in the future," Strickland said.

Gail faces another trial on Oct. 5 on charges that he solicited the murder of Gabriel Ponzio, a man in Florida whom Gail disliked. The murder never took place.

Did you notice that the article never mentioned the words armed violence, the crime for which I was convicted? This article was all about murder, and it made me look like the hitman the FBI and the ATF said I was for the past 15 years. And the nerve of the prosecution to ask the judge to consider certain of my taped comments when he sentenced me, without giving me the opportunity to use the tapes to defend myself. This is what passes for justice in a totalitarian regime, but it shouldn't happen in a democracy.

The article was accurate in one respect, though. Strickland was trying to show what I was planning to do because that was his entire case. He needed to believe I was such a piece of crap that I would kill someone because he fucked my girlfriend. No man on this planet would be less inclined to do that than me and I was more embarrassed than I was mad that he used that lie to establish my so-called motive. Strickland never once looked me in the eye. How could he, given that he knew I'd been set up. He also knew he didn't make a strong enough case during the trial to produce a conviction, but the weakness of Berkson's defense had bailed him out. And now, he wanted to put me away for as many years as possible.

Judge McKoski sentenced me to 14 years, more than twice the minimum six-year sentence he could have given me, but less than the full 30 years asked for by Strickland. The judge gave me 14 years for picking up a bag that contained one night's cocaine for two people, and an unloaded gun that I never asked for and didn't know was there.

25

THE DOUBLE-DOWNERS

GEORGE STRICKLAND'S TRICK was a good one but the truly remarkable part of his plan was its execution. He pulled the wool over the eyes of the court, my legal counsel, and the jury, because he needed to do it. To commit armed violence, you have to be armed with a dangerous weapon while committing a crime. Apart from picking up a bag that I had every reason to believe contained $100,000, what was my crime? If their whole case had been based on the contents of that bag, as it should have been, it would have been difficult to prove that I was guilty of anything other than picking up that bag. It's true that I was on tape asking for an 8-ball of cocaine, and I've already mentioned it, but I also told Grananta to forget about it if he couldn't get it within a day. They were able to leave that part out because, like me, the jury never had the opportunity to hear the tapes in their entirety.

Right after my trial, Berkson came to see me. Rather than apologize for losing the case, he decided to insult me. "I don't represent stool pigeons," he said, "but because it's you, I told the FBI that I would deliver the message. The FBI wants to talk to you about your friend." I looked at him and said, "Do you really have the audacity to say this to me?" and then I walked away.

In any case, trying me for solicitation to commit murder, as they intended to do, would have represented double jeopardy and

Strickland knew it. He would have presented the exact same case he presented at my Armed Violence trial, so I told Berkson to file a motion to dismiss the solicitation charge. In late October, 1992, Judge McKoski refused to dismiss the charges, but gave no reason why. That's when I cut ties with Dennis Berkson.

There's a footnote to this nightmare in regards to my attorney. Eight years later, Berkson called to tell me I was right in saying that he didn't contradict one word of the state's case. Somehow, it took him eight years to figure that out. He suggested I hire an attorney to motion the court for a hearing and he would testify to what he just told me. He probably thought it took him off the hook, kind of like he was confessing his sins in order to gain forgiveness.

In 1995, my third attorney filed for a new trial. He claimed I was denied due process and equal protection of the law because my first attorney didn't avail himself of several opportunities to protect me. Berkson failed to request that the State turn over the electronic surveillance tapes and the transcripts of those tapes. Since the crux of my defense would have come out during the cross-examination of the state's main witness, I was effectively denied my right to a fair trial.

My attorney pointed out there was no connection between the weapon and the commission of the underlying felony. The weapon was merely a prop, just like the ATF said it would be when they made their request to use it. It was never loaded, nor did I have immediate access to it at the time of the arrest. He also insisted that the State failed to prove that I even knew a gun was in the bag. He maintained that the State failed to make timely and appropriate disclosure of evidence to me through the Discovery process. It was only recently that I got access to my file and learned just how much information they withheld from me.

Strickland vehemently denied that prosecutors had withheld anything about Granata that my attorneys "were entitled to know at the time of the trial." He called it a "false allegation." Strickland was playing a game, only it wasn't a game to me, nor was it one I should have been playing in the first place. By withholding Granata's background and history from me, Strickland revealed the moral bankruptcy of Lake County's entire justice department. I should have been granted a new trial based on the prosecution's errors alone.

My new attorney asked for a speedy trial on the charge of Solicitation to Commit Murder. He motioned the court for permission to return me to Lake County Jail from Galesburg, Illinois so that he and I could begin preparations for the trial. The Illinois Supreme Court denied my petition, but ultimately it didn't matter. Seven weeks later, Strickland finally dropped the charge of solicitation to commit murder, but he gave no reason why. He had to drop the charge because his star witness, Joe Granata, had been arrested for murder a few months earlier in Cheyenne, Wyoming, where he was living in Witness Protection under an assumed name. Strickland sat on this information for four months before the news of Granata's arrest turned up in the Chicago Tribune.

At this point, Joe Granata was devoid of credibility. He didn't have any at my trial, either, but they wouldn't let me see his file. Now he was accused of murder and nobody in their right mind would ever believe a word out of this idiot's mouth. Plus, Granata had nothing to gain by testifying against me. Chicago was the last place he wanted to be because of all the enemies he made ratting people out. Strickland knew he could never bring that case to trial, much less win it, but rather than admit defeat, he said the charge could be reinstated at a later date. This SOB knew from the very beginning that I was being set up, yet he willingly and enthusiastically perpetrated a crime and a cover-up against me. He knew I didn't want to kill Ponzio, but he insisted I had killed Sam Canzoneri. That was his frame of mind when he conspired with the ATF to frame me and it's evidence of criminal intent on George Strickland's part, rather than mine.

What Lake County did to me wasn't an isolated incident. At some point in a democratic society, that kind of behavior was going to catch up with them, and it did, just not soon enough to help me. I haven't mentioned the name of Strickland's boss, State's Attorney Michael Waller, who signed off on his department's partnership with the ATF. He either created Lake County's culture of deception or he advanced it, because it was Waller's job to approve everything his prosecutors did. Rather than discourage their bad behavior, he encouraged it.

Waller was forced to retire after several Lake County convictions that relied on tainted DNA evidence came to light. "Echoes of the controversies that have marked his tenure will be heard in the courthouse halls after he's gone," wrote the *Chicago Tribune*. At the time of Waller's resignation, three other convictions were in jeopardy because Lake County hid DNA evidence that would have absolved the convicted men of guilt. The corruption in his department was endemic and though it ended up costing Waller his job, it didn't cost him his pension.

Corruption was deeply embedded in the psyche of Lake County's entire justice system. Highland Park police officers used to carry unregistered guns and bags of drugs in their vehicles for the sole purpose of planting evidence in order to make an arrest. They were able to justify this behavior, at least to themselves, by believing that anyone they framed had probably done far worse things that should have landed them in jail long before then. That was George Strickland's state of mind when he set out to frame me.

Michael Nerheim had served under Waller for the past seven years and was one of six candidates to replace him. "What troubles me deeply is the reputation that Lake County is gaining for being this hotbed of wrongful convictions," said Nerheim. "The job of the prosecutor is to seek justice, not just convictions." That's a refreshing sentiment, and one that Nerheim was wise to use in his election campaign. Waller's response was to double down, and he said, "I feel comfortable that we made our decisions based on the evidence we had at the time of the decision." Every prosecutor in the country has that sentence memorized and it effectively shields them from having to respond directly to claims of misconduct. Lake County had a long history of playing fast and loose with the facts. Facts can be manu-factured and truth can be ignored and Michael Waller and George Strickland did both of those things on a regular basis. They cared more about their conviction rates than they cared about justice.

In 2017, a 53-year-old man who spent 25 years in prison for raping a woman, was formally cleared of the crime. William Carini became the seventh convicted person to be cleared of rape or murder in Lake County since 2010. The prosecution had focused on Carini because he lived somewhat near the location of the assault and he had a criminal record. That's what passes for probable cause in Lake County, which helps explain what they did to me.

Once he was in office, Nerheim doubled down, just like Waller did. Surprise, surprise. Apparently, after you're sworn in, you have to drink the kool-aid. Nerheim said his office didn't plan on retrying Carini on sexual assault charges because of the "victim's preference against a retrial." At some point, Nerheim's office adopted a mission statement which I find laughable. "The Lake County State's Attorney's Office is dedicated to seeking justice with integrity by vigorously and ethically prosecuting criminal acts, with…unwavering respect for the rights of the accused…and providing exceptional and professional legal representation to Lake County and its elected and appointed officials, thereby promoting responsible and trustworthy government."

Like Donald Trump, prosecutors will never admit to making a mistake. Never! Refusing to admit they're wrong is a form of self-imposed blanket immunity which they use to justify their illegal or highly questionable methods. Prosecutors who admit to making a mistake come around about as often as Halley's Comet, which means you're lucky if you get to see it once in your lifetime. The bottom line is if the Feds want you, they're going to get you 95% of the time, and if your attorney isn't up to the task, you have no chance whatsoever.

26

HERE THEY COME AGAIN

I WALKED AROUND for 11 years asking myself, "How did this happen" and "What the fuck am I doing here?" I accepted responsibility for my first incarceration because I broke the law, but this was entirely different. Gabriel Ponzio initiated the scenario that put me in prison, but he walked free, even though he threatened to kill me and kidnap my son! What the hell is wrong with this picture?

I couldn't get Ponzio out of my mind for the longest time. There's no such thing as getting even, and I never tried to, but I had never been screwed like this before. For two years I was thinking of killing this guy in ways that no one ever imagined possible. I've known guys who've been whacked and I've known guys who did the whacking, and most of the time, guys didn't kill someone unless they had a good reason to do so.

Here's an example of what I mean. You're watching a movie where a guy is telling a wiseguy he's gonna pay him back the money he borrowed from him. In response, the wiseguy asks him if his wife and kids are still living on Cherry Street. In case you're not familiar with mobspeak, that wiseguy is threatening the man's family rather than making small talk. If a man had ever said that to my face, I would have killed him on the spot and that's why it took so damn long to get Gabriel Ponzio out of my mind. He had targeted my family and I would have walked into fire with this motherfucker, just like I was expecting to do with Joe Granata. It's a good thing I didn't know about his wanting to kidnap my son until I was behind bars.

A couple of years later, I sent my friend Carlo a copy of the transcript where Ponzio told Granata he might need to kidnap my son. Carlo was living in Florida at the time and I wanted him to know the circumstances which led to my incarceration. It was one thing for Ponzio to solicit my friend Ronnie's help in killing me, but it was another thing for him to threaten my kid. Carlo went to bat for me when he learned my life had been threatened, and I wanted him to know that Ponzio continued to pursue me even after I moved back to Chicago. After Carlo read those transcripts, he arranged a sit-down with Ponzio and his father at which he informed the old man of what his son had tried to do, and the damage it caused. Ponzio told Carlo he didn't know his conversations with Granata had been recorded and I believe that to be true. "What do you want him to do?" asked Gabe's father, who by this time was used to bailing his son out of trouble. Carlo told him that Gabe should go to Chicago and be deposed by my lawyers.

A few weeks later, Ponzio contacted my daughter. She arranged for us to have a three-way phone conversation so I could tell him how to contact my attorney. He was already in Chicago and when I asked him why he was there, he told me he was looking for a donor. "A donor for what?" I asked. He said, "My son has leukemia, and I'm trying to find a bone marrow donor." He told me his son was 26, which coincidentally, was the same age as my son. I said, "I'll talk to you another time, Gabe," and I hung up the phone. All of a sudden I felt the anger and frustration that had possessed me for the last two years leave my body. How ironic it was that this happened to Gabe's son after he had threatened mine.

I called my daughter back that night and her first words to me were, "Dad, I hope you're not mad at me." I said, "Mad at you for what?" She told me she called Mr. Ponzio back and offered to become a donor for his son. "No, sweetheart," I said. "I'm not mad at you. I'm proud of you." That's when I realized that nature takes care of itself. Gabe's son died from his leukemia and Gabe died of throat cancer a few years later. Before he died, Ponzio submitted a letter on behalf of one of my unsuccessful appeals. It read as follows:

> *To whom it may concern:*
>
> *I don't feel my life was in danger at any time.*
>
> *Mr. Gail never sued me for any money or anything.*
>
> *Mr. Gail never tried to get any proceeds on the house in question from me.*
>
> *I believe that Mr. Gail got caught in a miscarriage of justice.*
>
> *Whatever happened in Lake County, I'm sure Mr. Gail had nothing to do with it.*
>
> *Joe Granata called me on many occasions to talk about Mr. Gail and I told him to mind his own business, and that Mr. Gail has never bothered me or any of my friends.*
>
> *If Mr. Gail needs a job when he comes home I will try to get him a job where I work.*
>
> *This has been too long for Mr. Gail to be in jail for nothing personally known to me.*

In July, 1998, I was released from state custody, and was immediately taken into federal custody to serve the remaining four years of my parole violation at the prison in Pekin, Illinois. A year later, I was in a Peoria hospital for a prostate operation. I had a tube up my dick and IVs in both my arms when three ATF agents entered the room. "Kid," they said, "we're taking your DNA and if you refuse, I'm going to jump on top of you. We're not leaving here without your DNA."

They had gotten a court order to do this after finding hair in Sam Canzoneri's hands. They apparently overlooked this key piece of evidence for ten years but they seemed pretty damn certain that my DNA would be a match. Keep in mind that I was in a hospital gown and they were about to wheel me into major surgery. I said,

"Does it really take three ATF agents to swab the inside of a man's mouth? Go ahead and take my DNA, but when you find out it's not my hair, tell agent Delorto to come and see me." They swabbed me, but they never bothered to inform me of the results.

* * *

A few years after I got out, I went clubbing with a few friends of mine and I ran into two guys I hadn't seen in thirty years. They asked me if I would have a conversation with them and asked me to meet them at an after hours club. It was three in the morning when I got there. When I walked in, they waved me over to their table where they had a bottle of Jack Daniel's and a bottle of Sambuca. These guys belonged to a Chicago crew and they asked me if I could put the pieces together about Joe Granata and Gabriel Ponzio. I had a feeling they already knew that I could, and I did. It was the best seven-hour conversation I ever had in my life. We sat there from 3 a.m until 10 a.m. and I never dreamt that I could actually drink a fifth of Sambuca at one sitting, but I did.

One of their main concerns was whether Gabriel Ponzio had anything to do with my arrest. They wanted to know if he was aware that Granata had been working for the government and if he knew that Joe's phone had been bugged. I said no, and I gave them my reasons. I told them Ponzio was unaware of his cousin's involvement and that he did not know that Granata's conversations with him were being recorded. I also told them that Ponzio's interest in speaking with Granata was because he wanted to kill me over a lien that I placed on a house in which I had no legal standing.

They walked me to the door at 10 a.m. and I collapsed as soon as I saw the sun. They grabbed me before I hit the floor and laid me down on a couch where I was unconscious for the next four hours. They finally woke me when my cell phone began ringing every couple of minutes. Everyone who called was afraid that I had gotten killed because it wasn't like me to be gone for a whole night and day without telling people where I was. I drank so much that I was drunk for two days.

In the final analysis, I just happened to be involved with the wrong person at the wrong time, which is one of the recurring themes in my life. Sophia Sokorski's betrayal of me snowballed into something I couldn't have imagined was possible, and it was all set in motion 25 years earlier, on the day I had a chance meeting with Dominic Santarelli.

EPILOGUE

I'M THE LUCKIEST man in the world, a statement I'm pretty sure you didn't expect to hear from me. If I weren't able to say that, the past 40 years of my life would have been an unmitigated trainwreck. I've often wondered how I'm still here and it's because I never betrayed myself to myself. Rocky Marciano once told me something that I've never forgotten. He said, "Jack, a man must be a man regardless of the consequences." I believed that then and I believe that now. I'm the same person I was before I went to prison in 1979, and I've been that same person ever since. Still, it took a miracle for me to find happiness again.

I fell in love with Bonnie Sharkey the day I met her in 1977, and I never stopped loving her. When I got paroled in 2002, I heard that she was married and had a son, so I left it alone. Ten years later, I was invited to a Christmas party at the John Hancock Center on Michigan Avenue. My friends owned 200 Chestnut, a restaurant behind the Hancock that had valet parking. I went inside to say hello and to have a drink with them. Twenty minutes later, I left the restaurant through one of their revolving doors and that's when I got my miracle. At that exact moment, I saw Bonnie about to enter the revolving door. We saw each other at the same time and I said, "Are you shitting me?" And she said, "Are you shitting me?" It was surreal, and then some. We laughed and we picked up right where we left off after spending the previous 33 years apart.

I asked her where she was going and she told me she was going to see her friend Tony Ocean perform before she went home. "Oh no, you're not," I said. "You're coming with me." Bonnie was carrying a shopping bag and I handed my friend the bag and told him to hold onto it until I got back. I took Bonnie by the hand and we went to my friend's party at the Hancock Center, after which we came back to see Tony Ocean.

I couldn't stop apologizing to Bonnie. I always wanted to apologize to her after I chased her out of my life, but I never got the opportunity. I wanted to apologize to her mother and father too, but that ship had already sailed. I told her I didn't date married women and she smiled and said, "I don't either." She told me she was in the final stages of her divorce. Bonnie had to get home and I hailed her a cab, kissed her on the cheek, and asked her if she wanted to have dinner sometime. She kissed me on the cheek and said yes. We exchanged phone numbers and I called her a couple of days later. All the feelings I had came roaring back and my love for Bonnie was as strong as ever. This was either one of life's remarkable coincidences, or a kind of cosmic bonus for all the shit I endured over the years. I didn't care which one it was, but I was certain that nothing was ever going to keep us apart again.

Once in a while, Bonnie will mention the time I walked away from her in 1978. She wishes I hadn't done that but if I hadn't let her go, do you think anybody in her family would have ever talked to me again? I certainly didn't think so, because I would have felt the same way if the shoe were on the other foot. Life is full of decisions, some of which are extremely difficult, and those are the ones you have to make no matter what the consequences.

Bonnie and I got married at Chicago City Hall in 2015, a mere 37 years after we first decided to tie the knot. Three weeks later we went to visit her family at their vacation home on Put-In-Bay. They were selling the place and told Bonnie that she should look at it one last time before it got sold. That was fine with me because I hadn't seen the place in almost 40 years. One of her brothers-in-law told Bonnie he was taking us to a private dinner to celebrate our marriage after we looked at the house. We didn't know that the family had spent two weeks turning the place into a honeymoon suite for us. As we opened the door, we heard Sinatra singing, *The Best Is Yet To Come,* and Bonnie's entire family and many of her closest friends shouted, "Surprise!" They went all out to show their love and respect for Bonnie and I still don't have the words to describe what a classy move it was.

A few months ago Bonnie and I went to dinner at Carmine's in Rosemont. The place was packed and two guys at the bar looked like wiseguys. Bonnie asked them, "Do you know my husband? His name is Jack Gail." I don't know what made her ask the question but I'm glad she did. "Now, that's a man," said one of the guys. "Your husband's a legend." The guy mentioned I was a legend four different times, and after what I've been through, it was nice to hear that my original reputation was still intact.

Would I have done anything different with my life if I had the chance to do it over? Of course, but there's no point in trying to reimagine the past because you can't change it. I've told this story the way it actually happened and that's why I've named the names of the federal and state officials who pursued me solely because I wouldn't flip, rat or inform on anyone, not even the guy whose betrayal ruined my life. Those officials were the real criminals in this case. The Feds tried to break me like they were breaking a horse, but the only thing they broke was the law. They lost their souls in the process, though I doubt that they noticed or cared.

Made in the
USA
Columbia, SC